Wake Up Happy

PREVIOUSLY BY MICHAEL STRAHAN

Inside the Helmet:
Life as a Sunday Afternoon Warrior

·

Wake Up Happy

THE DREAM BIG, WIN BIG GUIDE
TO TRANSFORMING YOUR LIFE

MICHAEL STRAHAN

with VERONICA CHAMBERS

37INK

ATRIA

NEW YORK LONDON TORONTO SYDNEY NEW DELHI

ATRIA BOOKS   37INK

An Imprint of Simon & Schuster, Inc.
1230 Avenue of the Americas
New York, NY 10020

First 37 INK/Atria Books hardcover edition October 2015

37INK /**ATRIA** BOOKS and colophons are trademarks of
Simon & Schuster, Inc.

For information about special discounts for bulk purchases,
please contact Simon & Schuster Special Sales at 1-866-506-1949
or business@simonandschuster.com.

The Simon & Schuster Speakers Bureau can bring authors to
your live event. For more information, or to book an event, contact the
Simon & Schuster Speakers Bureau at 1-866-248-3049 or visit our website
at www.simonspeakers.com.

Interior design by Dana Sloan

Manufactured in the United States of America

10   9   8   7   6   5   4   3   2   1

Library of Congress Cataloging-in-Publication Data has been applied for.

ISBN 978-1-4767-7568-5
ISBN 978-1-4767-7570-8 (ebook)

I dedicate this book to all the people who have shaped me and continue to shape me to be the best that I can be. None of us do it alone and the best of me is really a reflection of you. Thank you.

If you want to be successful, it's just this simple.
Know what you are doing. Love what you are doing.
And believe what you are doing.

—WILL ROGERS

CONTENTS

Prologue: *Protective Gear*   1

1. What I Learned from Herschel Walker   9

2. A Line in the Water   21

3. Grit, Desire, and Discipline   31

4. Work Harder   41

5. Are You Your Worst Enemy?   49

6. What Did You Do to Get Better Today?   57

7. Fatherhood (Or, Thanks, Dad, for Setting the Bar So High)   67

8. Why Play *Should* Be the Work of Adults   75

9. The Power of Routines   81

10. Making It Right   91

11. What I Learned from Chris Martin and Coldplay   99

12. What I Learned from My Elders and Betters   109

13. Change Before You Have To   119

14. Curiosity and Visualization   135

15. Renovating One's Life   143

16. Come Prepared   155

17. Think Richly   165

18. Wake Up Happy   173

Epilogue: *Motivated to Find Love*   179

Acknowledgments   187

Appendix A: Strahan's Rules   190

Appendix B: Suggested Reading   193

Appendix C: The Playlist   195

PROLOGUE: PROTECTIVE GEAR

NOT TOO LONG AGO, I sat anxiously in a dark theater as the MC began his introductions. I was a bag of nerves. The MC didn't speak for very long, but it seemed to take *forever*.

"Come on," I wanted to jump up and say. "Let's get on with it!"

The longer he talked, the more nervous I got. At last, he began to wrap up his remarks.

"It's going to be okay," I told myself. "It's going to be okay."

Sure, it was a kids' talent show in North Carolina. Yes, my daughters were the ones performing, not me, but that didn't make me any less fidgety. Finally, the MC stopped talking and the curtains opened. Then my youngest girls, Isabella and Sophia, came out and sang "My Favorite Things" from *The Sound of Music*. "Raindrops on roses and whiskers on kittens." I love that song. And even though I was such a wreck, the girls sung beautifully. On the outside, I may have come across as cool and collected, but inside I was a mess.

All my life, people have always told me, "You look so comfortable," whether it was on the football field or hosting a television show or any of the other things I've done in between. If they only knew. The truth is, I'm a shy guy. I get nervous for myself and I get nervous when someone I love is out there on the line. But I've known ever since I was young how to take that nervous energy and turn it into positive energy. My goal in this book is to share with you what I've learned about developing a winning attitude and putting your most productive habits to work to craft the life of your dreams. I've had more than a few jobs, challenges, and personal transformations to which I've applied my philosophy, which I share with you in the pages that follow. Beyond my own experiences, throughout the book, I turn to other experts and people who've thought deeply and written about the power of positive thinking and transformation, from happiness expert Shawn Achor to Po Bronson, from Thor Muller and Lane Becker to Dr. Joseph Cardillo, an expert on energy management, to the figures who've meant so much in my life, from my dear friend Dr. Ian Smith to the late, great Giants coach Earl Leggett. In the second half of the book I talk specifically about how to use these principles not only to reach your goals but also to transform your attitude. In ways that may be counterintuitive, former professional athletes know a thing or two about transformation. Our career choices are, by definition, limited in duration. We can play only as long as our bodies, first and foremost, and our willpower allow us to. Then we have to reinvent ourselves.

Using stories from my own life and from those whose journeys have inspired me, I draw upon the power of positive thinking often. Take the time the producers of *Good Morning America* approached me about joining the team. I was scared to death. I was just getting my sea legs on *LIVE* with the talented Kelly Ripa and didn't think I could handle sitting at a news desk with esteemed journalists like

George Stephanopoulos and Robin Roberts. Then I had to ask my-self, "Well, am I not trying it because I'm afraid or is it because I think I can't do it?" After some reflection, I admitted to myself that I was afraid of trying and failing, and that wasn't a good enough rea-son not to give myself a chance.

That's a recent example of my working through my fear, but it's something I've been doing since I was a child, even when it comes to football. I don't remember the first time I ever held a football any more than I remember being handed my first bottle of milk. The youngest of six, with three older brothers and two sisters, I was surrounded by football enthusiasts. My brothers loved football. My parents loved football. Before I could walk or crawl properly, I could hold a football.

My brothers and I were always good at the game. It wasn't so much that we were innately talented as that we persevered. When I was seven years old, our family lived on an army base in Fort Bragg, North Carolina, where my father, Gene Strahan, served as a captain in the military. I still remember how excited I was to begin my first season on the Pee Wee Falcons team and the pride I felt in seeing that black-and-white uniform laid out on the bed. From the first time I donned a football uniform, I've loved the ritual of put-ting on the game pants with the built-in pads and the eyelet front. Then the shoulder pads with elastic bands and metal clips that make a distinctive sound when they're fastened.

I had watched my brothers do it a hundred times, but nothing had prepared me for the power and pride I felt the first time it was *my* turn. With my pads and my helmet on, I walked onto the field feeling like a gladiator, and an aerodynamic one at that. The sport may be brutal, but the design of the equipment is elegant, simple, and beautiful. Someday, if we ever get those flying suits that they used to talk about on cartoons like *The Jetsons,* I'm sure they'll be calling some of the engineers who design football uniforms. My team had a special chant, which I took pride in every time I sung it and which still makes me smile when I think about it. "What do Falcons do? Swoop, swoop, swoop." The fall I entered second grade, there was no day better than Saturday, when my mother laid out my uniform and I put on my equipment and I would swoop, swoop, swoop around the field.

One afternoon at a game, I made what I remember was the most amazing play of my Pee Wee career. An opposing player did a sweep around the opposite side and was headed for the goalpost. It was such an unexpected move that no one was even close to being able to stop him. He was twenty yards in front of me, but I ran him down and tackled him. The parents from our team went crazy, setting the bleachers afire, it seemed. My teammates were jumping up and down, screaming my name—all of which *terrified* me as I went crying back to the huddle. When I say crying, I don't mean that cinematic cry, just a few tears of happiness running down my cheek. I was doing an ugly cry: it was a bawling, snot-coming-out-of-my-nose, "Where's my mama? 'Cause I need her" cry. Thank God I had a helmet; it not only protected my head but also managed to hide the tears.

I learned something huge about myself that day. I loved making the play, but I did not like the attention. In time, I learned something else about myself: fear of being in the spotlight didn't stop me from pursuing what produced the fear in the first place; I pursued football nonetheless. Do I still get anxious? Of course. Intimidated? More than you know. As they say, *Show me the boy at seven and I'll show you the man.* But I've learned on the field that I can push through it. And I've been pushing through it ever since. The protective gear I wear these days is more mental than material. Gone are the shoulder pads and helmets. Instead, I employ what you can think of as attitude adjustments that help me play through the fear. I truly believe there's more power in your attitude than in your bank account. That's true for all of us, from the single mom struggling to build a brighter future for her kids to thought leaders, innovators, and entrepreneurs.

I have spent my entire career sprinting down that thin line between what's impossible and what's improbable. Along the way, I've learned how to turn self-doubt into an energy source and to metabolize fear into a result-producing adrenaline. When I was in college and really learning the art of football, I became so good at making plays and upsetting the other teams' offense on the field that the other teams began to assign *two* players to cover me instead of the customary one. The local reporters called this "Strahan Rules," as it was an uncommon practice that seemed to be implemented only for me. Throughout this book, you'll see my own live-your-best-life rules. Don't think about any of these as something that's being dictated for you to follow. But rather these rules are my way of giving you that extra oomph so you can carry your dreams all the way to the finish line. In a perfect world, I'd have ninety-two rules to match my jersey number. But in real life, I've found that you need only eighteen to get and stay motivated. I share those eighteen with you in the chapters that follow and sum them up in the appendix.

When considered together, my hope is that the "Strahan Rules" will help you transform your attitude so you can accomplish your goals. I was having a conversation with a friend recently. We were talking about how it is that some people seem able to drive toward their goals with so much joy, while for others it's struggle after struggle and setback after setback. All I know is that for as long as I can remember, I saw life as a game, a puzzle that I could solve again and again to get and achieve the things I wanted the most. I never—well, rarely—allowed myself to be overcome by doubt. I just kept telling myself, "I'll get there somehow." Did I know the exact method or route to achieve my dreams? Absolutely not. But I created a set of tools—rituals, ideas, formulas that helped me get from there to here—and that's what a lot of this book is about.

Even now when people say, "You're successful, you can have anything you want," I think, "What does that mean?" No matter what we accomplish, we're always searching for something else. I'm not talking about money or material things. I just think we have an innate desire, as human beings, to continue to achieve. Achievement, the quest and the process of doing more and being more, is the most powerful pathway to happiness.

Everything people ever want is because, at the core of it, they believe that it will make them happy. The goal could be a relationship, a house, or a career. But I've learned that happiness is, in and of itself, a choice you make every day. Every morning I ask myself, "How do I get to happy *today*?" Then I keep asking questions: Is happiness freedom? Is it honesty? Is it the passion you feel when you're doing something you love? Is it feeling wanted? Is it feeling needed? Is it giving and being of service? Or is it all of those things?

I've spent a lot of time asking myself these questions because, while I work extraordinarily hard and I play hard too, I want to make sure that I'm spending the limited time and energy I have on the things that make me happy.

Life changes every day, every minute. You're thrown things that don't seem fair at times; you're thrown things that you don't know how you're going to handle, or if you can even bear to handle them. But happiness is something that you have to find every single day. It's not a "Been there, done that." It's not "Well, I finished the happiness test and I got an A and now I'm moving on to the next thing." The quest for happiness is an ongoing pursuit, maybe the most important test of our lives. Because at the end of your life, if your stack of happy days is bigger than your stack of miserable days, then yours was a life well lived. It's that simple.

My goal with *Wake Up Happy* is to set you up for the win in your own life, no matter how many obstacles appear to be in the way. To quote lyrics sung by the legendary jazz singer Billie Holiday, "The difficult I'll do right now. The impossible will take a little while." So let's get started.

WHAT I LEARNED FROM HERSCHEL WALKER

Rule #1

Help can—and will—come from the most unexpected places.
Be open to everything around you.

MANNHEIM, GERMANY, was an awesome place to grow up. It wasn't a giant city like Berlin or Munich, but it was a big enough town and there was enough going on that we never got cabin fever. There was always something to do.

When I was thirteen years old, my favorite activity was to chase after my brothers and their friends. Wherever they went, I wanted to go too. My brothers, Victor, Chris, and Gene Junior, were fifteen, seventeen, and twenty-one, and I worshipped them. I had two older sisters as well, but it was all about my brothers to me. And then there was

our extended family. Because we were all so far away from home on
an American base, friends became family quickly. Mothers—many
of whom had neither the work visas nor the language skills applicable
to the countries in which they were based and therefore had time on
their hands—felt licensed to grab you by the collar and question you
as if you were a soldier gone AWOL, now facing disciplinary action:

> *Where's your homework?*
> *What are you doing?*
> *Where are you going?*
> *Where's my kid?*
> *Who's dating whom?*
> *Did I see your brother kissing my daughter? You know that girl is only*
> *fourteen; you better tell Gary that if he doesn't want Tanisha's father*
> *to have a talk with your father, he better act like he knows.*

This was Germany in the 1980s, so it was all Smurfs and gummi
bears at the Base Exchange, the shop near my father's office that
stocked everything we might need. But nothing you could buy in
a store could compete with my mother and her *Cake Boss*–level
baking. My mother and her friends made all of the classic deep
dishes from home: cherry pies, mixed berry pies, caramel apple wal-
nut pies. Then there were the cakes. Every mother I knew kept a
yellow cake with chocolate icing on a glass cake stand in her kitchen
in case her husband brought someone home for dinner, or an unexpected late afternoon coffee break, an unannounced guest, say a
high-ranking officer or a visiting American dignitary.

But that was just the standard. Like I said, these women had time
on their hands. So in addition to the yellow cakes they whipped up

from boxes of Duncan Hines procured at the Base Exchange, there was the more exotic fare: black chocolate lava cake or Earl Grey tea cake, not to mention all the German specialties. People always talk about the French and their bakeries. I've been to France more than a few times, but having grown up in Germany, I have to set the record straight for you: you can't tell the Germans a thing about making cakes. Forget about *Schwarzwälder Kirschtorte,* Black Forest Cake. That's nothing but a mess of chocolate, cherries, and whipped cream. Let's talk about some *Bienenstich,* Bee Sting Cake, a beautiful yellow cake confection with caramelized almonds and a buttercream filling. Don't even get me started on the *Berliner,* which are like jelly donuts—if jelly donuts were made in heaven, by angels. And then there's *Spaghettieis,* which is a bowl of German ice cream that has been put through some special spaetzle press so that the vanilla ice cream looks like a bowl of spaghetti, after which it's covered with a strawberry sauce, which is cooked to look *just* like tomato sauce, and then the sauce is covered with shaved coconut, which mimics Parmesan cheese. Proof positive that German ingenuity does not apply just to cars, people.

As you can tell, I spent more than a little time eating when I was a kid. My mother could cook, and she is, to this day, the picture of Southern comfort, easy grace, and hospitality. I'd get home from school and she'd wrap me in a giant bear hug.

"Afternoon, baby, how was your day?" she'd ask.

At thirteen, a lot of boys don't want to sit down and chitchat with their mothers. But I'd walk in the house, and the kitchen would smell like a bakery, and there was my mom—standing there like a female Willy Wonka—offering me the golden ticket of goodies every single day of the week.

She'd cut me a big piece of just-baked streusel and pour me a cold glass of milk, and you bet I'd sit down for thirty minutes and tell that woman anything she wanted to know. I'd tell her about how Mrs. Polans was a nice teacher, but Algebra 1 was so freakin' hard, I didn't know how I'd make it to Algebra 2. Or about how Mr. Adlersflügel, who taught our German class, cut himself shaving each and every day. He'd come to class with little pieces of toilet paper all over his face. My mother would laugh so hard at my impression of Mr. Adlersflügel, done in animated, exaggerated German. "Oh, bless his heart!" she'd say. "He must be single, because no woman would let him walk out of the house like that." My mother didn't have a mean bone in her body, but she loved to hear funny stories about our teachers and the other families on base, and I loved to make her laugh. Louise Strahan's laugh is just like her baking: all butter and sugar, with just the tiniest dash of salt.

My friends and I did our best to increase awareness about the game of American style football. We would play with whoever expressed an interest. And when we tired of football, we would go to a friend's house and play Atari. But what I really loved to do was hang out with my brothers.

One afternoon I was following the older kids. My brothers and their friends kept calling back to me, "Bob! Bob! Keep up, Bob!" I didn't think anything of it. My brothers always called me Bob. Sure, it was an odd nickname, given that my name is Michael. But not any odder than what my friends were called by *their* big brothers.

That day, as I was huffing and puffing my way up that twelve-foot fence, my brother's friend Anthony came up behind me.

He said, "You know why they call you Bob, right?"

I shrugged. Who knew why my brothers did *any* of the things they did?

He turned to me sympathetically. "Bob stands for Booty on Back," he said. "They call you that because you're fat."

When he told me what "Bob" really meant, a name that my brothers had been calling me for *years,* I was stunned.

I close my eyes and I can see myself, plummeting four feet down to the ground slowly, so slowly that I have the time to ask myself the question again and again:

Am I fat?

Am I fat?

Am I fat?

I hit the grass with a thud, and while I can feel the bruises coming up on my back, my neck, my arms, feel the cuts and scrapes on my bare legs, I'm hurting far more on the inside than on the outside.

Anthony looks down at me. He is still hanging on to the fence. "Hey, man," he shouts. "You okay?"

I nod yes. Then I say it as loud as I can. "Yeah, I'm okay."

Once I see Ant has cleared the fence and gone running toward the field, I dust myself off, and with real, hot tears on my face, I take off in the other direction—toward home and my mom.

Louise Strahan has many gifts, but lying is not one of them. If Germany had ever been invaded during our time abroad, and the security of our base and the nation relied on her powers of subterfuge, we would've all been sunk.

"It's a simple question, Mama," I asked. "Am I fat?"

My mother looked as hurt as I felt as she tried to dodge the truth. "Oh no, baby," she cooed. "You are not fat. You are *husky.*"

I rolled my eyes.

She then gave me a hug and cut me a piece of freshly baked pecan pie. (I know it's illogical that I'd follow the most devastating insult of my young life with dessert, but *come on.* I was thirteen. I was not about to say no to pie.) As I sat at the table, my mind worked on the problem. My father always said, "Show me the baby, not the labor. Tell me about the solution, not the problem." But to come up with the solution, I needed to define the problem. There were fat kids at school. We all knew who they were. But my *friends* never called me fat. When I looked in the mirror, I didn't see a big boy. So how was I going to fix it when I couldn't even see it?

That night, when my dad came home from work, I asked him if I could talk to him in his bedroom, privately. My dad is not my mother. My dad will tell you the truth, even if it hurts.

"Dad," I asked. "Do you know why my brothers call me Bob?"

My dad nodded his head yes.

I took a deep breath in and forged ahead, just to get my mind fully up to speed with what was going on.

"Dad, am I fat?" I asked.

My dad didn't look pleased to tell me, but he did anyway. "Yes, son. You could lose some weight."

I was crushed. "What am I going to do?"

My dad shrugged. "Eat less. Exercise more."

"Okay," I said.

Then my dad did what he does so well: he gave me the little bit of extra insight that helped me figure out how to get the job done.

"It's a simple formula," he said. "But it's not an easy one. You're going to have to eat a *whole* lot less. And you are going to have to exercise a *whole* lot more."

I started watching what I was eating. That's not the easiest thing for a thirteen-year-old growing boy to do. But the fact is, I'd been going to town, breakfast, lunch, and dinner. My mother's food was so delicious, I would typically go back for seconds and thirds even though I knew I was full. Now, instead of having two plates of my mom's broccoli-and-rice casserole, I'd have just one. Same thing with dessert—just one helping, and I aimed to make it a small one. Being older, my brothers Victor and Chris hardly made it home for dinner most nights. So there was only my mom, my dad, and me home most of the time. It pained my mother to see me eat less. She'd get an expression on her face like a dog lover watching a stray being kicked on the street. It seemed to her a form of child abuse not to fill my plate to the top and then refill it again.

Sometimes she just couldn't help herself: "Baby, Mama's got butter cake for dessert. And ice cream. Let me cut you a nice big piece, you've hardly been eating at all."

Luckily my father was always there to step in. "Louise," he'd say lovingly but sternly. "You see what he's trying to do. Just let the boy be."

Because I was a kid and my metabolism was through the roof, I began to lose weight quickly—even with regular samplings of my mother's desserts. But the thing that made the biggest difference was the exercise. I'd purchased a Jane Fonda workout tape—yes, tape, on VHS—and every day after school, I'd pop it in.

I know it might be hard to imagine me, six-foot-five former pro-ball player, on the floor of his parents' living room, sweating it out with Jane Fonda. But you have to remember. This was 1985, and Jane Fonda was at the forefront of a fitness revolution. I saw the commercials for her tapes on television and what seemed clear was that they worked.

The first day that I brought the tape home and popped it into the VCR, my mother stood at the doorway of the living room, cheering me on. "Go ahead, baby, you work that booty off," she said, with a smile.

I was glad my mom wasn't going to supervise my workouts or join in, because this is the thing: the Jane Fonda workout videos were unexpectedly hot. Not since I'd seen Jennifer Beals in *Flashdance* when I was twelve had I seen so many good-looking women walking around in nothing but leotards, leg warmers, and the occasional off-the-shoulder sweatshirt.

The music is vintage eighties pop: lots of keyboards, synthesizers, and drum machines. And the way the video starts out, it's almost as if the women are in a club—a club where they walk around in their leotards or, as in the case of the blonde who is front and center, a sports bra, a skimpy leotard, and a white visor—to keep the sun out of her eyes (indoors nonetheless). After they greet each other, they start throwing their legs up on the ballet barre. There are two guys and about fifteen girls—which seemed like the kind of odds I liked.

I've always been a guy who doesn't just listen to music. I get into the lyrics. And the lyrics of the opening song to the Jane Fonda workout tape seemed to speak directly to me.

There's so much more to you than meets the eye.
There's so much more in you, you're going to try.

From the beginning, I found the workout challenging, but the distraction of the pretty girls helped me get through it. Because my brothers had teased me about my bubble butt, I paid special attention to the glute exercises. If Jane said do twenty leg lifts, I did fifty. If she started with fifteen fire hydrant kicks, then I'd pause the tape and do an extra twenty-five. I was literally trying to work my butt off. It worked. I started at the beginning of the school year, and by Christmas I was trimmer and fitter than I'd ever been.

That year, the Dallas Cowboys signed a player named Herschel Walker. I hadn't grown up in Texas, but the Cowboys were a big part of our household because my parents are Texans through and through. Unlike a lot of pro athletes, Herschel never bragged about the hours he logged in the weight room. Instead, he had always been—since he was a kid my age—into exercises that used his own body weight. I was amazed to learn that at the age of twelve, Herschel had weighed only one hundred pounds and was just five feet, three inches tall. He'd had the exact opposite problem from mine. Instead of being "Bob," he'd been the puny guy that nobody ever picked for sports. Creating his own routine of push-ups, sit-ups, pull-ups, and quick sprints, he'd built his body up into a muscle machine. By the time he'd reached ninth grade, he was a high school football all-star and weighed in at an impressive 185 pounds—all muscle with impossible-to-beat speed.

Herschel didn't have a video like Jane, but he had a book called *Herschel Walker's Basic Training.* I'd lost enough weight that my brothers stopped calling me "Bob," but I didn't want to stop. Herschel's book seemed like the perfect next step. I saved up and bought that too. I began to get serious about building muscle.

One of the things that Herschel talked about in his book was how, as a kid, he would do push-ups and sit-ups during the commercials on television. So in addition to doing the Jane Fonda workout three days a week after school as soon as I got home, I added in Herschel's moves during the commercial breaks of my favorite shows.

My father had always been an active dad. When I was six years old, he was one of the commanders of the 82nd Airborne Division, the paratroopers at Fort Bragg. He'd let me come with him on training runs with the troop. If I ran the whole way, I'd get a big bottle of Gatorade at the end. My dad would have to force my brothers to run, but I just loved following behind the troops as they sweated it out in the sun, singing "I don't know what you've been told . . . But 82nd Airborne came to rock and roll." I might as well have had a sign around my neck that said, "Will run for Gatorade." But it was more than that; it was a way for me and my dad to be together, to be active, and to work out.

As much as I loved our time running together, between the ages of nine and thirteen I stopped playing organized sports and began to spend more time eating and sitting around watching television. Hence the weight gain that led to the "Bob" nickname. Now, with Jane Fonda and Herschel Walker in my corner, my father saw how serious I was about getting into shape and he started working out with me every day. My dad is a reader. He'll buy a computer, and before he even opens the box, he will sit and read the manual cover to cover. He wants to know all there is to know on any given subject. A decade before any of us had ever used the term Google, my father would research a subject exhaustively.

So when my workouts became his latest project, my father spent weeks doing the research to make sure he best understood how to train a teenage boy like me. He read every muscle and fitness magazine he could lay his hands on. He created specific weight training programs that I would follow and he would log. On the weekends, we would jog together for miles. It was on those runs that I got to know who my dad really was.

I also learned that help can and will come from the most unexpected places and people. When I was a boy, it was Jane Fonda and a football great, Herschel Walker, long before I ever had an inkling I'd one day play the game professionally myself. Consequently, I make a point of not making assumptions about people and staying open to the possibility that alliances might come in the most unlikely packages.

2

A LINE IN THE WATER

Rule #2

Sometimes you'll catch the big fish, and sometimes you won't,
but without a line in the water, you don't stand a chance.

M Y DAD, GENE STRAHAN, was born in Weirgate, Texas.
Weirgate's a town in East Texas, established in 1917 by the
Weir Longleaf Lumber Company to house the employees
of that company. Home to magnolia, black cherry, and white ash
trees, Weirgate is a workingman's town. But my dad didn't get to
enjoy the scenery much, because he was like a wood-hauling John
Henry. From the time he was really young, he worked for the lumber company. Here's the thing about my dad, though; he must've
been born with a pretty high happiness set point, because he never
let his present define his future. He always knew that he would do
more than haul wood, and he trusted, step by step, that he would
figure that next thing out.

There's a little family lore about how my parents met, and it goes like this. Word is that my father had a crush on my aunt, but when he found out she was spoken for, he ended up switching his affections to my mom. Everything happens the way it's supposed to, because Gene and Louise Strahan have been together ever since. They fell for each other hard, and no matter how rough the road, they never fell out of love. They do more than stick together. They make each other laugh; they make me laugh, and if you ever had the chance to meet them, they would make you laugh too. Mom is Lucy to Dad's more straight Ricky Ricardo.

My dad always begins his stories with "Let me tell you something."

As in, "Let me tell you something, your daddy was a big-time boxer in the military. I could knock a man out before the first bell. Back in the day . . ."

Then my dad will stand and throw his dukes up, like he's going to show me—his six-foot-five son—a thing or two.

My mother will shut him down. "Oh, Gene, *please,* that day is long over. The only person you're liable to hurt these days is yourself."

It's pure comedy to me.

My mother was a star athlete when she was a girl. She ran track and played basketball. My father, on the other hand, played a little football . . . "little" being the operative word. With no football scholarship in the offing, my dad decided to join the military with his best friend from high school, Mr. Arvelle.

My dad and Mr. Arvelle were so poor that they each had only one non-uniform outfit respectively, and they used to swap the two they had so it looked like they had more clothes than they did.

With a military career on track, my dad asked my mom to marry him, and she said yes. He was only twenty to her sixteen. But they were in love, and beyond making each other laugh, they figured that was all they needed. The rest they would figure out one step at a time, one day at a time.

By the time my dad was in his early thirties, he and my mom had five kids, and I was on the way. He knew that in order to raise us the way he wanted to, he needed to go back to college and become an officer. My dad took a leave of absence and enrolled in the ROTC program at Prairie View A&M University. Barely hiding their cynicism, everyone said, "No way. Look at that old man in the ROTC." But my dad didn't care. He went through the program and graduated magna cum laude. And then he went back into the army as an officer. I was just a baby when my dad graduated from college, but throughout my own development, the story of how he persevered always made a big impression on me. I thought, "There's no reason why you can't do something, even if it seems hard, even if it seems impossible." If anybody had an excuse not to go back to school, not to try, he did.

One of the most popular courses at Harvard as I write this is called Positive Psychology, and it's a course about happiness. Over decades of studying happiness, the professors who teach this course have discovered something that my father seemed to know instinctively. Being successful doesn't make you happy. There are a lot of people in corner offices with big job titles and big perks who are very good at what they do, but they're not happy. Being rich doesn't make you happy. (Although I won't lie, not having to worry about money is *nice*.) Being famous doesn't make you happy either. Anyone who's watched even a little bit of reality TV can tell you that. Rather, according to Shawn Achor, one of the Harvard happiness professors, it's the attitude with which we pursue our goals that gives us our biggest boosts of happiness. Achor says, "Happiness is the joy we feel striving toward our potential."

I've seen that joy in my dad time and time again. It was in his face and in his heart when he was a thirtysomething college student and folks were laughing at him, calling him "Old Man River." He had it when he left his job hauling pulpwood and joined the military in the first place, with only one change of clothes to his name. My dad's not afraid to bet on himself. Win or lose. He takes joy in striving toward his potential, and he taught me to do the same thing.

My father took an incredible amount of pleasure in being a dad. Though busy with responsibilities as a major in the military, he spent every free moment he could with us. When I was in elementary school and he was stationed in Fort Bragg, North Carolina, we'd spend our school breaks driving in the family camper cross-country, home to Texas, where our extended family still lived. On the weekends, we'd go hunting and fishing, and if we kids couldn't go, if we had a school event or something that precluded our going, Dad didn't go. It was almost as if he knew that there would come a time, and that it would come sooner than he wanted it to, when we kids wouldn't want to hang out with our parents. So he treasured the time with us. It wasn't ever anything he said. It was the way his eyes lit up when we walked into the room. The way he called out to us when we were all piled into the camper. It was his voice, the way he modulated it from commanding officer to doting dad. He had a range, and on one end he was stern and authoritative, the voice of a disciplinarian. At the other end of his vocal range there was this tone he used with us children and with my mom that resonated with love.

While I was in the midst of my Jane Fonda period, my father retired from the military and opened a moving company in Germany.
He and my mother liked it in Mannheim. As a result, like so many
other former military families, they decided to set up shop and stay
in Germany. I think the decision was due, in no small part, to the
fact that they liked raising their kids abroad. I can't imagine what my
life would be like, or what I would be like, if my parents had pulled
up roots and I'd attended a public school in Texas during the middle of the crack epidemic of the 1980s. Mannheim was safer, more
cosmopolitan, and a world away from the troubles that faced many
of the urban and poorer rural communities back home.

Despite his decades of military service, because my father was
retired, he wasn't allowed to let me attend the American school on
base. Or rather, if I did attend the school, tuition would be fifteen
thousand dollars for me and another fifteen thousand dollars for my
brother Victor, who was in tenth grade, money that my parents sim-
ply did not have. So they explored other options.

I began ninth grade at a more affordable new private school that
was just starting up. Unfortunately, it was a mess and, even at the
age of fourteen, I knew that no good would come of my going to
that school. I came home and told my parents, "I am not going to
that place." They moved me over to another, more affordable private school: Mannheim Christian Academy. My parents worked
hard. By the time I was in high school, my dad had a trucking business and my mom worked driving a truck too. But their number-
one priority was always our education. I liked school, but it would
drive my mother crazy that I used to take my time with my papers.

I'd say, "Mom, I need to borrow a book from the library."

She'd ask when the paper was due.

I'd tell her Friday.

She'd say, "Let's go to the library on Tuesday then."

I'd say, "No, Thursday is good."

My mother would give me one of those big Texas harrumphs. "Boy, if you've got all week to write the paper, then why wait until Thursday?"

I'd shrug and say, "Thursday is good."

I'd get the book on Thursday, hand the paper in on Friday, and then when I got the paper back, my mother would look at it and say, "I can't believe that teacher gave you an A."

I'd smile. "See, Mom, you've got to relax."

She'd say, "I'll say one thing. You're nobody's dummy."

Because my older siblings were largely out of the house by then, I got a lot of one-on-one time with my father. Back in the States, we used to go hunting, but my dad had had a change of heart about hunting by the time we moved to Europe. He woke up one day and said, "Kill an animal for sport? For what reason?" Just like that, he decided, "I'm not a hunter anymore." I love that about my father. He's not someone to just dig in his heels and keep doing things the same way over and over again. He's thoughtful. He considers things. And he always taught me that you're not a man because you stand your ground; it takes a lot of character to say, "I used to do things this way, but I've learned. Now that I know better, I'm going to do better."

He ended up getting rid of all his guns. But his love of fishing never waned, and I'll always remember the fishing trips to Spain we used to take. My dad bought this used Mercedes camper in Mannheim, and I swear it was the slowest thing since human beings ever put an engine in a box and plopped the thing on four wheels.

We'd drive at five miles an hour from central Germany to Spain, listening to the oldies along the way. There was this one song I never got tired of listening to:

Then along came Jones.
Tall, thin Jones.
Slow-walking Jones.
Slow-talking Jones.
Along came long lean lanky Jones.

En route to Spain, as we camped in one park or another, my dad would heat up pork and beans at each campground. At times he'd make the most amazing chili. Then when we got to Extremadura, in western Spain, it was as if we had traveled to the other end of the world. Do you remember that old Brad Pitt movie *A River Runs Through It*? Our lives at times resembled a scene out of that movie— just me and my dad in this huge national park and nothing but forest for as far as you could see. There were three reservoirs—Serena, Orellana, and García de Solí—and two giant rivers flowed from these.

The world's biggest barbel fish was caught in that region. The lakes are teeming with carp and bass. It was world-class fishing; it still is. But I knew that for my father, these trips were a gift beyond sports: a way for us to connect with each other and nature, but also to really get out and see the world. Even as a major in the army, my father never made a whole lot of money. But he could get in his old camper van and drive his son to Spain. My father gave me the kind of experiences that as a poor kid growing up in East Texas, he never imagined he would be able to give his son.

I watch people play the lottery and I know that they are thinking "if" and "only." If I could only win the lottery, I could send my kid to college. If I could only win the lottery, I'd take my wife on a cruise or a European vacation. What I love about my father is that he sat in an East Texas shotgun house where, more often than he would want, they dined on air pudding and nothing pie, and he didn't buy a lottery ticket. My father leaped toward the nearest available brass ring—the military, and then, through the GI bill, a college education. Once he became an officer and a stint abroad became a possibility, he leaped for that too. Then after he and my mother had raised five children, they looked at me, number six, and thought, "What can we do for this child? How can we expand his world?" My dad looked at everything within reach and thought, "If I take a week's vacation and we pile up the camper, we can get from Germany all the way through France to Spain and all of that fine fishing." He made something out of nothing.

A recent study found that American employees left more than 50 *billion* dollars in unpaid vacation time on the table last year. The amount of vacation time taken is at its lowest in four decades. Our grandparents took more vacation than we do. That's crazy. What could you do with your kids, your loved ones, your friends, in five days with a car and a couple of hundred dollars in the kitty? How creative could you get? How much fun could you have? How many memories could you make? Those are the questions my parents asked, and the answers they found, sitting over our kitchen table late at night with a calculator and a calendar, created a sense of possibility that shapes my life to this day.

You couldn't tell me anything when I was out in a boat in Spain with my dad. I felt like the big man on campus, years before I went to college. My father created a sense of adventure with every road trip, and he gave me his undivided attention. He'd ask me to talk about my dreams; then he'd push me to dream a little bigger. A lot of the time, once we got seriously focused on the catch of the day, we wouldn't talk at all. But even when we sat in silence, I benefited from my father's presence. I'd seen him at work. He was a major in the army and was respected in every room he entered on that base, but out in the boat, by giving me the gift of his time and attention, my father reminded me he was more than his job. He was a father who loved spending time with his son. Even if we didn't catch anything, it was still relaxing and peaceful just to be out on the water. Some of our best memories were from those days we didn't catch anything or even get a little nibble. We would sit there for hours, waiting for the real bite that never came; but we had each other.

It's a good way to relax, and maybe it's a lesson on life. Throw the line out in the water, and every once in a while you get a little nibble that gives you hope that a big one is coming. That "sometimes" is all you can hold on to. Sometimes you'll catch the big fish, and sometimes you won't. At least having your line in the water gives you a shot.

Looking back through the long lens of time, I know this to be true. People think broadcasting is an easy and natural extension of a pro-football career. The truth is, there are hundreds of pro athletes who retire each year, looking for their next gig. When I left the NFL, I put a lot of lines out in the water, as I discuss in later chapters. Not all of them were successful, including a little-known sitcom I did called *Brothers*. It was canceled after just one season. Some people might consider that a failure. But in my mind, it was a line in the water. And if nothing else, I had something to strive for—and the happiness experts will tell you that that alone breeds its own kind of joy.

3

GRIT, DESIRE, AND DISCIPLINE

Rule #3

Grit, desire, and discipline are free and the only equipment you need to start just about any endeavor you'll set out to do.

WHEN I WAS in the ninth grade, Herschel Walker, my hero from the fitness books, came to Germany. My friend Kevin's father, Mr. Smith, drove us from Mannheim to Heidelberg, so we could meet him. I remember that during the entire week, I alternated between being extremely pumped and absolutely terrified that something would go wrong and I wouldn't get to meet my idol. What if Mr. Smith had to work late and couldn't take us? What if we got to Heidelberg and they had oversold the tickets and wouldn't let anyone else in? (As a military kid, I had a deep understanding of the rules and knew that maximum occupancy was no joke in safety-conscious Germany.) And then when I met him, what was I going to do? I wanted him to autograph my book, but after that, what? What was the one thing I could say or ask him that would matter?

Finally, the day of the event arrived and it all went off without a hitch. Herschel's tour was being sponsored by Kodak, so when we got there, we learned that every kid would have an opportunity to take a Polaroid with the star. I distinctly remember standing next to him, smiling for the camera, and the moment before the orga- nizers rushed me off the stage. I was proud that I'd lost some of the weight before meeting Herschel Walker, that I could walk up onto that podium as Michael Strahan, not as "Bob." I hadn't just done the exercises in Herschel's book; I'd tried to absorb the sense of *possibility* that emanated from each page. In his book, he'd written that as a kid, he'd transformed his body with "grit, desire and disci- pline as my only equipment." Having flexed my own inner strength to change my body, I began to wonder what untapped resources I could tap to change my life.

My dad and I would stay up past midnight together on Mon- day nights to watch NFL games on the American Forces Network. Eventually, I began to use our VCR to tape other American sports programs that came on in the middle of the night. The next day I'd come home from school and pop in a tape and watch *Sports Tonight* on CNN. I taped and watched all the games. When I was sixteen years old, my dad said, "I think you want to play football."

This was surprising to me because I hadn't *played* football since I was a little kid. That would be akin to turning to a sixteen-year-old girl who liked to watch skating on television and saying, "I think you'd like to be a competitive figure skater." She may have the passion and some innate skill, but she would have so many years of training to do, so much catching up, that it would be virtually impossible.

But my dad saw something in me, something he may have seen in his older brother, my uncle Art, who had played two years of professional football back in the 1960s. Uncle Art played for the Houston Oilers in 1965 and the Atlanta Falcons in 1968. My dad knew that I lacked the technical skill to play football competitively, but he had also seen how determined I was once I set my mind to something.

It wasn't just the weight I'd shed with that Jane Fonda video or the muscles I'd sculpted by my careful studying of Herschel Walker's training book. When I was in seventh grade, I had this ridiculous hand-me-down bike. It looked like Frankenstein had found all these random pieces and put them together to make a bike. My father refused to buy me a new one.

"The bike works!" my dad bellowed every time I brought up a new bike.

My mother wasn't much help. "It was good enough for your brothers Victor and Chris."

I'm a total mama's boy, but sometimes her attempts to *pretend* like I'm not her favorite child got on my last nerve.

But the thing is, I didn't just want a new bike. I wanted a top-of-the-line BMX. I took out the catalogue and passed it to my father.

He slammed it on the kitchen table so hard he almost knocked over his morning coffee. "Twelve hundred dollars? Boy, are you out of your mind? My first car cost less than that."

My mother looked up from the pot of rice she was stirring and said, "And every bicycle on the road was faster than that car." Like I said, Lucy to his Ricky.

Then my father made what I am sure he thought was a sucker bet. "How about this? If you can earn half the money, then I will pay for the other half."

It was the beginning of my school summer vacation, and I am sure my father thought that after eight weeks, I'd have fifty dollars to show and that I'd settle for a new Huffy and be happy to have that. But that's not what happened.

First, I tried babysitting, at which, admittedly, I failed miserably. The parents would go out, not far, just somewhere on the base. They would come home, and I'd be asleep on the couch while the kids were still awake!

Next I started cutting grass. In these military apartment buildings, it's barrack after barrack. Everybody's got a big yard and the grass grows fast in the summer. But it's the military, so an overgrown yard is not tolerated. I went door to door and offered my services. By the Fourth of July, I had signed up over a dozen yards by offering to "cut your lawn once a week for twenty dollars." I was meticulous in my work, and even though it was hot and I was miserable, I kept going. I had done the math in my head and knew that enough lawns, with enough repeat business, would get me my bike. I'd internalized what Herschel Walker had said about grit and discipline. The Friday before Labor Day, I showed up at the dinner table with six hundred dollars, mostly in fives, tens, and a lot of dirty, wrinkled ones.

My mother gave me a big hug. "That's my baby."

My father took the stack of bills and began to count them carefully. I don't think he ever intended to spend even a hundred dollars on a kid's bike, much less six hundred dollars. But when he counted the money and saw it was all there, he said, "A deal is a deal. Just give me a couple of days to pull together my share."

The day that we drove into town to buy that BMX bike was one of the happiest in my life. I learned that you've got to work for everything and you've got to work hard. It also taught me that it's different when you're spending your own money as opposed to spending someone else's. And I think it taught my father that although I was the baby of the family, I was also maybe the most determined kid in a bunch of strong-willed Strahans. I think it was the bike as well as the five-mile morning training runs that made my dad think that if I got a chance to play football, I could be good. Maybe even great.

After a lot of late-night conversations, my father came up with a plan. He would send me to Houston for the first semester of my senior year in high school. I'd live with my uncle Art, play for the local team, and if all went well, it would be enough to get a college scholarship.

There were, to my mind, a lot of things wrong with the plan. First and foremost, I was seventeen years old and close to my parents. I didn't want to move back to the United States without them. I had also met a girl named Wanda and we were in love. Still, I knew what a football scholarship would mean: a free ride at college and maybe even a chance at the pros. I owed it to my parents. I owed it to myself to give it five months and try it out.

．　．　．

I went to Houston in June, as soon as school let out. It took everything I had not to cry when I said goodbye to my girlfriend, Wanda.

She was a student at Mannheim Christian Academy. Her father, like mine, was career military. Her mother was half German and half French. Because we had grown up in the same way, in the same places, we shared similar values. And she was beautiful. I couldn't believe that she wanted to go out with me, that she loved *me*. I had transformed my body, and yeah, I looked like a standout athlete. But inside, I was the kid who liked to play cards with my mother and father on a Friday night instead of attend a keg party at an off-base apartment. Inside, I was still the youngest in the family, a boy who looked up to his older brothers, the kid who grimaced at the thought that not only was my nickname "Booty on Back," but it had taken me *years* to figure it out. I was shy, and although I liked to joke around, mostly I liked the quiet time of talking one-on-one. Wanda knew all of that and she loved me. And now I was going to Houston, leaving her in Germany, and hoping that when I got back, she'd still be mine.

The year was 1988, and R&B music was full of young men singing their heart out about love. Every song reminded me of Wanda. Keith Sweat singing "I Want Her." Bobby Brown crooning, "Don't Be Cruel." Billy Ocean urging a generation of fine-looking women to "Get Outta My Dreams, Get Into My Car." And Terence Trent D'Arby hoping for love in a "Wishing Well." I made mix tapes of all of my favorite love songs and played them over and over on my Walkman the whole ten-hour plane ride from Germany to Houston. How could it be that when I finally got a girlfriend, a *really* beautiful girlfriend, I had to leave her in Germany for six whole months? By the time the plane landed, I knew every word to every song on those mix tapes.

I hadn't been back to the United States since I was nine years old.

At seventeen, I felt hopelessly naïve. I remember arriving in Houston and being shocked by the neon "DRUGS" signs at every strip mall. I thought, "The drug dealers are so bold here! They just set up shop in the strip mall and the police don't do a thing." It wasn't until my aunt took me into the "DRUGS" store to get some Tiger Balm that I realized that what I thought was a narcotics warehouse was what we called, in Germany, an *Apotheke,* or apothecary.

Football off-season began right away. I'd met the coach only once before I started to play, and honestly, I think he looked at me as this big black kid whose uncle had been in the pros, and he thought, "He can do this." In truth, I understood neither the game nor the technique. I had the work ethic, and I had the desire, but I didn't have any skills to speak of. I had to figure it out.

I know that I didn't look like your typical German exchange student. But from my first day, I felt more like a foreign student than an American. The entire student body of Mannheim Christian Academy was smaller than a single grade at Westbury High School in Houston. I'd thought that the kids I knew in Germany were the usual mix of studious and reserved and loud and rowdy. But the loudest, rowdiest kid at our school couldn't compare to the kids in my new school. At Westbury, the kids drove cars, went out all night, talked back to teachers. There was no core of military parents and the kind of oversight that comes when you know your family is connected to the U.S. government. Growing up on and near the American bases, one internalizes a sense of service: your parents are on a tour of duty, and in some ways so are you. But at Westbury, the kids made their own rules, and the only sense of duty was to their homeboys or homegirls—or at least that's the way it seemed to me.

It didn't help that I was homesick. My aunt Jean and uncle Art are two of the loveliest people you'll ever meet. I loved spending time with my cousins, Andre and Taylia. But it wasn't the same as being in *my* house, with *my* mom and dad. When you're close to your parents, no one can take their place. I couldn't shake the feeling that I didn't belong, so I just withdrew into myself. I would go to school, go to practice, then come home and *stay* home.

The season started, and I got my first taste of playing on the giant stage that is a field in a huge stadium in Texas, where football is everything. When you have a high school stadium that holds thirty thousand people, then you know—it's more than just a game. Beyond the physical aspects, part of my training involved developing a way to manage the fear inside while thousands of people were cheering and booing, watching and judging. Because the stakes are so high for football in Texas, I got a crash course in dealing with the pressure.

I soon learned in front of all those people that I sucked—hence the boos. Looking back on my skill level during high school, I realize I had no idea what I was doing. Most of my peers used to watch football on television and try to emulate their favorite players on the field. They knew the game inside and out. In the 1980s, my dad and I had this routine every week in the fall: we would go to bed as early as seven P.M. on Monday and get up at three A.M. to watch football on television. In the United States, the games they were watching were known as *Monday Night Football,* but in Germany, where we were living, it became *Tuesday Morning Football.* I'd spent many years doing that, but the difference between playing football and watching it on television is like the difference between watching a guy drive a race car on TV and trying to drive that bad boy yourself. You think, "I know how to drive. He's just going fast and going in circles." But you get into that car and all of a sudden you get it: he's not just going fast, he's going *really* fast, and every hairpin turn, every fun-looking donut requires a mathematical level of precision. That's the way it is with football at its highest level—there's just so much *technique*. I had no idea how important a sack or a tackle for loss was. It was all a challenge to me.

Football practice was a special kind of torture, because as much as I loved the sport, when I was up against eleven guys who'd played their whole lives, I had trouble holding my own. Yet as my dad had seen, and as I would continually prove to myself, I'm not someone who's afraid of a challenge. I try to see an obstacle not as an issue or a problem, but rather as something interesting to solve. Getting good enough to be an asset to the team was a puzzle to solve. So I listened more than I talked, paid attention to the guys who were the stars, and studied the playbook the same way I had studied Herschel Walker's fitness book. I also learned to convert the boos into a kind of juice that would drive me. I'd go straight to the place of "You're doubting me? Let me show you what I can do."

I also paid attention to my uncle, who taught me how to work and how to be tough. When I was in Houston, he'd take me in the front yard and show me pass-rush drills, how to use my hands. He'd hit me a little too hard, but I wouldn't tell him. He played a big role in my development.

On top of all this, there was the social aspect. Though I was friendly enough with the guys on the team, I didn't really make friends. I missed Wanda. I didn't even talk to other girls. I just kept my eyes on the prize of getting incrementally better, of getting good enough, contributing enough to the team, so that when I went home at Christmastime, I'd have a college scholarship in hand.

For six long months, I played and studied the game. The days were long and the nights were longer, lonelier. The guys who played with me, the coaches who worked with me will say that I came over from Germany and I *killed* it. They'll say that they knew I was a star. But that is more good-hearted amnesia than it is actual truth. The semester that I played in Houston, I was never very good. But I got good enough that one school, Texas Southern University, a Division I-AA program, offered me a scholarship. It's kind of like somebody buying your house. You don't need a hundred offers. You just need one. Using all the grit, desire, and discipline I could muster I got my one chance.

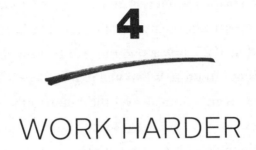

WORK HARDER

Rule #4

It's natural to have doubts. But hit pause before you out-and-out quit.

WENT HOME TO GERMANY for Christmas, and it was as if the reel of my life had been one of those black-and-white films that had been colorized. It was as if I'd been locked away in some sort of American high school football purgatory, and then finally, finally, they let me come home. Home was my dad, ready to take me fishing. Home was my mom, cooking up a storm. Home was Wanda, still in love, still beautiful, still wanting to be with me. Just as important, I came home with a huge sense of pride and accomplishment. Bringing home a full-ride scholarship to an American university was, for both my parents and me, bigger and better than any gift I could put under the Christmas tree.

Spring semester at Mannheim Christian Academy was easy

breezy. I knew where I was going to college. I had a great girlfriend whom even my parents loved; Wanda quickly became like another daughter to them. I graduated second in my class. It's no skin off my nose that there were only two kids in my graduating class. For six months, I had a blast. Then it was time to get back to work.

Texas Southern University in Houston is a historically black college started in 1927. It was one thing to be in high school with all the guys from Houston. When you're in college at a historically black school, with guys from all over the country, it's very different. When you grow up on a base in a foreign country, you look at being American as a point of pride. You don't focus on skin color because your tribe, so to speak, is the group of other Americans abroad, and we supported each other. Coming back to the United States, to a school where everybody had the same ethnicity and a lot of people weren't interested in or open to people from other backgrounds, was a culture shock.

The year before I arrived at Texas Southern, Spike Lee had released his seminal film *School Daze,* about historically black colleges. The film had been wildly popular, due in no small part to the hit song from its soundtrack, "Da Butt." ("Hey pretty, pretty. When you get that notion, put your backfield in motion.") But the film had also been controversial, particularly among black college administrators, who didn't like what they saw as dirty laundry being aired. Some schools banned Lee from appearing on campus. But for me, in 1989, *School Daze* was like an anthropological field guide to attending a historically black university. Every college has its own factions and cliques, but the groups I saw at Texas Southern had their roots in the history of black colleges: There were the politically conscious students who wanted to uplift the race. There were the black fraternity brothers who were often the sons of the black middle-class elite, and the black sorority sisters who not only came from similar social backgrounds as the fraternity members but also tended to be "light-skinned" and have a certain hair type. Athletes had a kind of free pass to mingle among any of the groups, which was helpful because it gave me time to observe and figure things out.

My father would say, "Don't get sidetracked by the obsession Americans have with black and white. People are people." At Texas Southern, we had only one white guy on our team, a kicker named Ted Leva. I still talk to him all the time.

As had been the case when I was in high school, the other guys on my team and the players on the opposing team seemed to know so much more about the game than me. I didn't get the rules on the field and I didn't get the lifestyle off the field. The coaches had run us to death, at least I thought they had, and I didn't think I was contributing. We were losing all the time. To make matters worse, I never connected with the social life at Texas Southern. At that time, socially, I felt more European or German than I did American.

With neither friends nor an understanding of the game, I was ready to give up. When it was time to go home for Christmas vacation, I had no intention of ever coming back. I packed up every last thing from my dorm room because I was not returning. I emptied my room—lamps, clothes, pillow, sheets, right down to the last pencil and eraser. I was going home to stay.

Christmas came and went in Mannheim, and so did New Year's Eve. Mid-January was approaching.

"Isn't it time for you to go back?" my dad asked.

I tried to make my voice a little deeper so that my dad would know that there was *conviction* behind my words. Then I told him, "I'm not going back to Texas."

My dad had run whole platoons of special troops. At eighteen years old, I wasn't going to out-man him. He made his voice even deeper than mine. And when he spoke, he spoke slowly. "So . . . what are you gonna do?" he asked.

I shrugged. "My brothers work for you. I want to work for you in the trucking company too."

My father paused, and he clasped his hands together and took a deep breath. He could see that I had talent, but he could also see how lonely and homesick I was. I sat looking at him, nervous and scared about what he might say next.

My dad took another deep breath and then he said, "No, Michael. Listen to what I'm asking you. What are you going to do for *you*?"

After several sleepless nights, I decided to return to the university. My father had a vision for me and a plan, but he couldn't do it for me. Your parents can't take care of you forever. I had to do it. I came back to school, not because my father wanted me to, but because *I* wanted to. Other people can spark a vision for your life, but until you can hold that dream in your own head and your own heart, it's never going to come true. We think that we have to sell others on our worthiness, but the first—and most important—person we need to convince is ourselves.

That realization didn't make it any easier when I got back to my dorm room in Houston. Again and again I'd come back to the room after a hard class and an even harder practice and muse aloud that my dad must've been dreaming to think that I could be a college standout, much less play professional ball. During long weekends and other school breaks, I'd watch as the other guys went home while I sat in my dorm room by myself. Home for me was five thousand miles away. Even now, September in Texas smells like sadness to me. For four long years, I found myself there in the autumn heat, chasing my football dream, thousands of miles away from everyone I loved.

Yet, slowly, I built my college career as a starter and pass rusher: I made fourteen and a half sacks as a junior, nineteen as a senior. Because Texas Southern was not a college powerhouse, I reasoned I just had to work harder to stand out. The upside was that I got a lot of personal attention from the coaches that I probably wouldn't have gotten at a bigger school. The defensive line coach was a guy named J.W. Harper. Like me, Harper had a good idea of what it was like to feel out of place at a historically black college. He'd grown up in Shelbyville, Tennessee. In the early 1970s, he was one of the first to integrate Middle Tennessee State. That school is famous for their football team, and currently they boast sixteen conference titles. J.W. was the first African-American to wear a Blue Raider uniform. He reminded me of my dad, so I not only took his coaching seriously but felt proud to know him.

He could see that I was self-motivated and that despite my size—I was already six-four and over two hundred fifty pounds in college—I was smart. He used to tap his head and say, "Keep that motor running, Strahan. I can see the wheels turning." Under J.W.'s coaching, I reconnected with that impulse that earned me that bike. I already had my desire. I rekindled my grit and discipline and developed the mental toughness that I would need to play the game professionally. I realized that even the most determined among us have setbacks. Pull back before you drop out. Pivot, don't quit. Easier said than done, I know.

J.W. helped me to see that my speed was what would set me apart from other defensive ends. Remember how I ran down that kid in the Pee Wee league? I can still see myself on a hot September day, three o'clock in the afternoon and it's ninety-five degrees. I'm running drills and J.W. is shouting out commands, "Make the first step quick, Strahan! Run, keep the other guy off your feet."

Off the field, J.W. echoed the advice that I had always heard at home. "Don't be a skirt-chaser or a hell-raiser," he would say. "Work hard, stay out of trouble, and maybe you might make it to the NFL." During my junior year at Texas Southern, John Singleton released his groundbreaking film *Boyz n the Hood.* By that point, I no longer felt like the German foreign exchange student. The scenarios in the film were very familiar to me from four years in Houston: the drive-bys and the 40s, the long stretches of road with nothing but pawnshops and gun stores. I'd never been around guys who used drugs before, but at Texas Southern, I saw it. The great thing about my dad was that he told us early and often that no good ever comes of drug use. You never hear, "Oh yeah, that guy started snorting cocaine and things got better and better." I was lucky that we'd had those conversations. I always managed to be independent. I've never been intimidated into doing something that I didn't want to do because other people were doing it. J.W.'s advice resonated with what I'd learned from my dad.

Slowly I started to emerge from my shell socially. I spent a lot of my free time with my friend Corey Johnson, who was a linebacker.

On Saturday mornings, instead of sleeping out a bad hangover, we worked with kids at a YMCA near campus.

I also decided to get a car so that I could get off campus more often. I heard that someone on campus, a friend of a friend, was selling his used car cheap. I called my parents to ask them to help me buy the car.

I said, "Hi, Mom. There's a car for sale and I really want it."

My mother said, "Have you seen it?"

I was nineteen years old and not the most savvy consumer yet. "I don't need to see the car, Mom. It's a car, so it doesn't matter what it looks like. It's better than walking."

My mother sighed and said, "Don't you think you need to look at the car first?"

I could tell from the pots clanking that she was in the kitchen, cooking up something delicious. But I tried to stay focused. "I want the car, Mom."

My dad made the arrangements, and I got the money to buy the car. It was a royal-blue Festiva with a bright-pink stripe. The paint job wasn't my favorite, but the real problem was that the car was tiny. I'm a big guy. No sweat. I thought maybe my parents would help me sell the Festiva so I could get a bigger car. Maybe one of my cousins in Texas would take it off of my hands. My mother was not having it.

She said, "Well, take the front seat out and sit in the back and drive. You will drive that little car until you buy your own. I told you to go look at the car first."

I'll never forget that one day I was getting into the car and some cute girls were watching me. They said, "Hmmm, that must be his mama's car or his girlfriend's car that he's riding around in."

I said, "One day I will be able to get any car I want. You will never say that about me again. It will be my car and it won't look like this." Once again, the negativity, the boos, only fueled my desire to achieve.

I made it back home to Germany for Christmas vacation each year in college, but the other holidays I stayed at school. Uncle Art was nearby and I'd visit him, but I missed my parents and friends back in Germany. Easters and Thanksgivings were the toughest. I would sit for hours feeling sorry for myself. Eventually, I decided that instead of saying, "I'm alone for the holidays," I was going to say, "I've got extra training time that the other guys don't have."

I would put on my roommate's weighted shoes and run the football stadium steps. I would run the empty streets. I would run laps around the gym and go back into the stadium and run the steps again. When I would call home, my father would encourage me and say, "Son, it will pay off in the end." I knew that his words weren't hollow. He'd gone to college in his thirties with a passel of kids to support, well past what most people consider the time to pursue a college degree, especially back then. There's no one who can tell my father something he doesn't know about working hard to get what you want. Dad used to say, "Just thinking about it ain't gonna make it happen. Wanting it to happen ain't gonna make it happen. Expect it to happen and work every day to make it so." I've used that work ethic in every serious pursuit I've aimed for.

5

ARE YOU YOUR
WORST ENEMY?

Rule #5

Too many of us count ourselves out before we even give ourselves a chance. Do the work. Be excellent. You'll find your
place, and it may just be where you least expect it.

T WAS MY senior year at Texas Southern and I was on my way to
making it to the pros. I was also about to become a father. The
night my daughter Tanita was born, I lay in my dorm room bed,
waiting for news. I was fortunate enough to have a single ten-by
sixteen-foot box to call my own, which also meant I didn't have to
explain to a roommate the call I was expecting. I was twenty years
old and I was going to have a baby.

My fiancée was back home in Germany, and I wished I had figured out a way to get home for the birth. I knew that she was sur-

rounded by family: her mother and my parents, who loved her as if she was their own child. I prayed that she didn't feel as alone as I did that day.

From the moment she told me the news, we promised each other that we would never use the term "mistake." No child who was so loved could ever be considered a mistake. We got engaged. Wanda would have the baby. We would get married. But every month when she sent me photos of her belly getting bigger, it felt like photos from my future. The future where I was a grown-up, settled down, and ready to be a dad.

We had always planned to be together, but I had hoped to have a pro contract in my hand when I asked her to be my wife. Knowing that I had a child on the way made my longing to go pro cut even deeper. Every practice, I rushed harder, knowing that now Draft Day wasn't just about the glory of getting into the pros, of becoming one of those pros I used to read about every chance I could back in Germany, where I'd pore over the magazines, idolizing them. I would soon have a wife and child to support. An NFL contract would help me start off my family life on a more secure path.

The knock on my door was so soft I almost didn't hear it. "Michael, are you in there?" he whispered.

Nathan was a scrawny freshman who worked part-time in the Athletics Department as their work-study assistant. He was from Seattle. "Mercer Island, to be specific," he would frequently remind people. I often thought that maybe if he'd been exposed to a little more sun, he wouldn't have been such a small guy. Nathan was smart, though. He not only photocopied our playbooks but was the guy who would pull tape and research on our biggest opponents. The work he did was crucial to the few games we did win. I liked him. And one of the things that I liked about him was that he was one of the few guys who remembered that I did not like to be called "Mike." Nathan always called me Michael.

I threw my legs over the side of the bed. The standard dormitory bed was about four inches too short for me, so I always slept and napped with my legs bent. Getting out of bed, for me, was synonymous with the kind of leg cramps that would take minutes to shake.

"Hey, Nathan, what's up?" I asked as I threw the door open.

"They called," he said cryptically. There are a lot of secrets in the athletics office of a Division 1 college. Nathan was good at keeping them. I don't know where he is now, but if you told me he worked for NASA or the National Security Agency, I wouldn't be surprised. Even as an undergraduate, Nathan had a PhD in Hush Your Mouth.

What I said was "Cool." What I wanted to say was "I'm a dad. I'm a dad. I'm a mother★★★★ing dad."

The summer before, when I'd gone home to Mannheim, was when Wanda had told me the news. The first person that I told was my father.

"I would've liked for you to have a few more years without the responsibility," my father said. "The timing is not ideal, but this is not a tragedy. You are about to become a father, but you are still my child. As long as I have breath, I will do for you what I can."

"Thanks, Pops," I said. But the words were too small to convey everything I felt in that moment. I couldn't undo what had been done. My dad didn't say much that afternoon, but his few well-chosen words reminded me of the steadiness of his presence and assured me that his wisdom, his guidance, and his love were always mine for the asking. I had leaned on him my entire life. And I could lean on him still. It didn't make me ready for fatherhood, but it made me ready to give it my best shot.

When we got home that afternoon, my father jumped in and said, "Louise, Michael has something he wants to tell you."

My mother stood at the stove adding butter to a pan of mashed potatoes. She didn't even turn around. "Wanda's pregnant."

I looked at my father, who shrugged. I knew that my mother and Wanda were close, but I didn't believe she'd tell my mother before she told me.

"Did she tell you?" I asked.

My mother smiled at me knowingly and gave me her best "Boy, don't be a fool" glare. Then she said, "I've had six children. I know a pregnant girl when I see one."

All of those memories came rushing back at me as I walked across campus to the Athletics Department with Nathan. It was 1992. I didn't have email. Nobody I knew had a cell phone. I didn't want to use the dorm phone, so my coach had given me permission to make an international call in his office. Nathan deposited me at J.W. Harper's office and muttered, "Good luck, man." Then he walked away.

I walked into the coach's office and sat at his desk. I felt immediately a little bit more grown-up, sitting on the coach's side of the desk. I took out the number that Nathan had jotted down, Wanda's hospital room. Her mother answered the phone and quickly passed it to Wanda.

"How are you, baby?" I asked, trying to picture the girl I'd known since I was seventeen as the mother of a child, *my* child.

"I'm good," she said. She sounded tired but happy.

"And how's the baby?"

"She's a girl and she's beautiful."

I willed myself to breathe. Deep breath in. Deep breath out. It's the simplest thing to do, but the easiest thing to forget when you're in the thick of things.

We talked for a few minutes more and then I said goodbye. I would be home by Christmas, but Christmas felt a long way away. As I walked back to the dorm room, I whispered my daughter's name as if she was close enough to hear me, as if I was holding her in my arms and rocking her to sleep for the very first time. Tanita. Tanita. Tanita.

. . .

Wanda and I got married, and she, along with the baby, moved to Houston. I moved out of the dorm and into an off-campus apartment with my young family. I know some of the guys thought I'd caught a rough break: not even twenty-one and already a dad. But I hadn't been happy being the single guy in the dorm. Being with Wanda felt like being home.

Being a father was new, but honestly, Wanda did all of the hard work. She changed the diapers and handled the late-night feedings. She warmed the bottles and did the never-ending loads of laundry. I went to school and played football. "Played" football is of course a euphemism, because by now the sport was much more than a game. I had *wanted* to be great, to make it to the pros and see how far I could go, but now I *needed* to be great. Football was everything. There was no plan B.

I became such an unrelenting defensive end that other teams began to assign two guys to cover me, a practice of double-teaming that local reporters started calling "Strahan Rules." This was the first time that I learned if you're good enough—if you work hard enough and you're unrelenting, you can make your own rules. You can literally change the game. I was selected to the All-America First Team and set a school record of 41.5 career sacks. My trophy mantel became crowded with awards like Division Defensive Player of the Year and Associated Press First-Team College Division All-American.

Then came Draft Day 1993.

The day all of my dreams would start coming true. I was home in Houston having a Draft Day party with my family and friends. The plan was that I would be drafted by the Dallas Cowboys. Jimmy Johnson was the head coach of the Cowboys, and he had let me know he wanted me. Local media were camped out at our house to catch the moment when the call came. My mother, who was in from Germany, took care of my baby, Tanita, who had just celebrated her first birthday. They say that babies tend to look more like their fathers in the first year, but then the mothers' look starts to creep in. At one, Tanita was a little mirror of her mother's delicate beauty. I loved being her father, loved being the one she crawled to for bear hugs and tickles.

Wanda and I sat on the couch, watching the draft on television. Texas had been my home for the past four years. My parents were from Texas. My relatives with whom I had stayed during my senior year of high school were from Texas. I was sure that the next step for me was playing for the Dallas Cowboys, it just felt so right. Jimmy Johnson had flown me and a handful of other prospective players to Dallas to meet the executive team and a few of the players. I was told that the Cowboys would pick me in the first round, and just to make sure that I understood how serious their commitment was, the Cowboys had sent a scout with a jersey for me to throw on when the big announcement was made.

Then the unexpected happened. The Cowboys traded their thirtieth pick for another selection. The scout got the call and literally *snuck* out of my house. I couldn't believe it. On some level it was inconceivable, but anyone who's ever watched a pro draft knows that there's always the unexpected move. I willed myself not to panic. Deep breath in. Deep breath out. I was good. It took teams of guys to stop me. Deep breath in. Deep breath out. I reminded myself that Strahan's Rules meant that I was going to get drafted, but by whom?

The year before, the Giants used their first-round pick in 1993 in the supplemental draft to get a quarterback named Dave Brown, which meant that they couldn't pick until second round. They picked me. The Giants had one of my football idols, Lawrence Taylor, L.T., a man who had literally rewritten the rules of the game playing my position. When I got the call from Dan Reeves, my first thought was "Why do you need me? You've got L.T." My second thought was "It's cold up there." I remember watching Giants games as a kid, watching the clouds of smoke come out of their mouths while they were playing and thinking, "I don't want any part of that." But I also knew that New York was one of the biggest stages an American football player could ever command. It was like that old joke about Carnegie Hall. How do you get to Giants Stadium? Practice, practice, practice.

So much of my life has been about things coming full circle. As life would have it, I would end up cohosting *NFL on FOX* with the same Jimmy Johnson who had passed on me in the first-round draft pick. Not too long ago, he told me, "I'm mad that I didn't draft you when I had the chance. But I didn't know you'd be that good."

There's not a person alive who's not experienced the sting of rejection. There's always somebody—in the workplace, in your personal life—who passed on you because they didn't know that you'd be *that* good. Other people's choices and actions are entirely out of our control. But how we view ourselves is entirely up to us. Too many of us count ourselves out before we even get a chance. We can be our own worst enemies. Do the work. Be excellent. You'll find your place, and it may just be where you least expect it.

6

WHAT DID YOU DO TO GET BETTER TODAY?

Rule #6

The juice is worth the squeeze. When we push ourselves, sometimes it hurts. But when we realize we've got more to give, we put ourselves in the position of getting more.

EVERYTHING ABOUT NEW YORK scared me. The Giants flew me out and put me up at the Marriott Marquis in Times Square for three days. I didn't leave the room. I was afraid of all the people in Times Square. Afraid that I'd look like a country bumpkin and get robbed. Though six-foot-five, I was naïve on many levels. But I wasn't a fool. I knew what I didn't know. And I knew that Houston was like a kiddie amusement park compared to New York.

Finally, Stanley Ralph came and got me. Stanley's the little brother of actress Sheryl Lee Ralph, and at the time he was working as a liaison for my first agent. "You can't stay in the room the whole time," he urged me. "Just walk around. Walk over to Rockefeller Center. Up to Central Park, down to the Empire State Building. It's a free trip. Go see something." So I took a good look at the map that the hotel clerk handed me, memorized it like it was a playbook, then folded it up and put it in my pocket, praying to God that I wouldn't have to break it out and look like a tourist.

I was walking down Sixth Avenue when I saw a face that I recognized. It was Tom Bosley, the actor who'd played the dad in one of my favorite television shows when I was a kid. *"Happy Days,"* I remember thinking as I smiled at him. That must be a good sign.

. . .

Just as there is no manual for parenting, nobody tells you how to be a first-year rookie on an NFL pro team. By your senior year of college, you think you've got it all figured out. You've got the moves. You've got the accolades. The local media know your name, and then on Draft Day some big-league coach calls and says, "Come play on my team."

I walked into the locker room of training camp, and it was as if it was three in the morning in Mannheim on a Tuesday morning and I had fallen asleep on the couch, trying to stay up to watch *Monday Night Football.* There, standing just a few feet before me, were all the gods of the gridiron that I'd grown up watching on television.

I'll never forget being in the locker room for the first time. We were getting our physicals, and one of the last guys to come in and get his was the legendary L.T. He didn't walk in the room so much as he *glided* into it. I wanted to ask him for an autograph. That's how much I respected and looked up to him.

During training camp, the great Phil Simms walked up to me and said, "Hey, Michael." And I felt all the blood rush to my face. I remember thinking, "Oh my God, Phil Simms just spoke to me."

I didn't know how I was going to compete alongside guys like that. There was no amount of ego that could pump me up into thinking that I knew even a smidgen of what those men knew. No breathing technique advanced enough to give me the self-confidence. So I kept to myself and focused on what had gotten me my ticket to this particular party: developing my body, developing my craft. There would be no victory dances—at least not the first year. I had this recurring dream that I intercepted a pass and got to the end zone and danced. In the dream, because I did that silly dance, I missed a major play the next day. I felt like the dream was trying to tell me something important: dancing like you own the place would be a setup for a slipup.

The Giants used to hold their training camp at Fairleigh Dickinson University. There's a long tradition in training camp, where you're sitting around having your meal and you hear someone clink on his glass with a fork. Then he'll call out your number and say, "Sing, rookie."

For years, the rule of this particular gentle hazing was that you had to sing your school song. I don't know what happened to that tradition. Maybe players got tired of hearing school songs or maybe some senior player realized that there was much more comedy in having you sing something else. But by the time I got to the pros, the rule was that you could sing anything *but* your school song.

For days, I watched my fellow first-year players embarrass

themselves. You think you know a song until you have to get up and sing it in front of eighty-five tough guys. I watched three-hundred-pound guys warble about their achy breaky hearts. Some guys tried to be cool and spit a little rap. They learned the hard way— rapping is a lot harder than it looks. You may be an NFL player with some swagger, but that doesn't make you Snoop Dogg or Ice Cube. You better sit down before we start calling you Ice Melt.

When one of the players tapped his glass and said, "92! Sing, rookie!" it was finally my turn. I'd learned enough from watching the other guys to know that the more you hemmed and hawed, the worse it was for you. The more miserable you seemed, the more likely that they would pick on you again and again. So I played it cool and dug out something from my junior high school repertoire: New Edition's "Can You Stand the Rain." I thought all I'd have to do was sing the chorus like I was in church on a Sunday and every-body would be singing along with me. So I found a point to focus on and sang:

> *Sunny days, everybody loves them.*
> *Tell me, can you stand the rain?*
> *Storms will come, this we know for sure.*
> *Can you stand the rain?*

One of the senior players gave me a little guff: "That was sweet, cupcake." But then I heard the five sweetest words a guy can hear during training camp: "You can sit down, rookie." And I never had to sing during training camp again.

There was a lot of horsing around, but at the end of the day it was all hard work, and increasingly no one expected more out of me than I did. I was determined to help the team the first year in some way. I knew I wasn't an every-down player going in, but my goal was to learn the defensive end position and get stronger, so that eventually I would play every down.

Earl Leggett was the Giants' new defensive line coach. A big guy with a thick accent, Leggett was the first NFL player from Jacksonville, Florida. I liked him right away because I knew that he was a guy who understood what it meant to hustle. He was so poor as a kid that his high school coaches had to buy him socks and shoes to practice. He left home with all of his belongings packed in a paper bag, to play football at Hinds Community College in Mississippi. When he became a standout on the Chicago Bears, he was an integral part of the defense that earned the team the nickname "The Monsters of the Midway."

By the time I met Earl, he'd already transitioned from history-making player to legendary coach. He coached Howie Long for ten of his thirteen seasons with the Raiders. According to Howie, "Playing for Earl is kind of like playing for John Wayne; there is no middle ground. He was tough, hardheaded, and unrelenting, and still is. I've often kidded Earl that the only reason that it took me two years instead of one to figure out how to play in the National Football League was because I couldn't understand a damn thing he was saying. Playing for Earl was not for everyone. He took you to a place mentally that you weren't aware you could get to."

Earl liked that, in a lot of ways, I was a blank slate. "Michael hasn't played a lot of football, but he reminds me of several players I've coached," Leggett said. "Players who came into the league without a lot of experience but became outstanding players through hard work. Guys like Howie Long, Greg Townsend, Sean Jones—

a pretty good list. Michael can be as good as he wants to be; it depends how much he puts into it and how much I make him put into it." I was all for being shaped and molded by Mr. Earl Leggett. I came into the NFL a white wall. I said, "Paint me however you want and I will work to make it happen."

I'd learned a few things in college, but there was so little nuance to my game back then. If you'd asked me to define the purpose of my role as a defensive end, I would have said, plain and simple: "Get the guy with the ball." Everything Earl and my coaches taught was new to me. I wasn't changing bad habits; I was making new ones. And because I was very much aware of how much I didn't know, I was listening to every single word that Earl Leggett said.

A lot of guys come in from college and high school with a certain amount of success doing things their way. Those same guys become really resistant to learning and changing. It's kind of like someone is stuck in the seventies or eighties and they're dressed a certain way. You look at them and you say, "Yo. It's not 1986, man. Take that Jheri curl out." You've got to realize that things have changed.

The average NFL player gets to play just three years in the league. Rookie salaries are on par with top law school graduates or top MBA graduates, but those guys can count on thirty or forty or even more years of employment. Imagine what a young lawyer's life would be like if that lawyer knew that in three years, she or he might be out of a job. That the lawyer would have to totally reinvent her or his career in a new field (and I have a lot to say about career reinvention in the second half of the book). I was always aware of the ticking clock. I never took a moment of my first year for granted. That's why I knew I lucked out when I got Earl Leggett as my coach.

Without him, I wouldn't have been in the league very long. I would have been that average player with three years before I was out.

Earl Leggett took me under his wing, but this is the thing: he knew I was willing—and *happy*—to do the work—and there was an excessive amount. His goal was to tire the defensive crew out from the drills and exercises we did *before* we joined the rest of the team for afternoon practice. He's one of those believers in repetition. If you do it so many times, it will come off automatically. He was absolutely right. He had a lot to give. The only thing he required from you was that he needed you to come ready to work.

The other players, the guys on the offensive team, who didn't work with Earl, would feel sorry for us because they would see how hard we were working. "Man, I'm glad I'm not in that group," they'd let it be known. He was that kind of coach. But this is also where I started to develop a friendship with Howie. Howie let me know how much I could learn from Earl, that Earl wasn't the coach you're glad you *have,* he's the coach that—one day—you'll be glad you *had.*

The work took a toll on me. Every day I'd come home beat up physically, broken down mentally. But the next morning, I'd wake up feeling whole and stronger. It's no exaggeration when I say that at the end of the day, Earl taught me everything I know about football. Pay attention to detail, the specifics of the techniques; develop a mental toughness.

Earl's motto was "I want to get you as tired as I can before practice starts. And I want to test your bloodliness. I want to see what your momma and your daddy are made of. I'm going to test your grandparents and your great-grandparents and see what they're made of. I'm going to work you so hard that if they weren't made of much, you ain't going to be made of much."

Often when I was lying out on the field, gasping for breath, hoping for some kind of natural disaster, for the ground to just start quaking so that I could get up and go the hell home, I thought of something my mother always told me. She would say, "Don't ask anybody to give you anything, just ask them to give you an opportunity. You can be anything you want to be, just know you're going to have to work for it." I knew that was what Earl was offering me, the opportunity to do the work that this would take me where I wanted to be in this sport.

I would see a similar factor at work with my friend Kevin Hart. A lot of people think of him as an overnight sensation, but he is someone who has always shown up and done the work. More than a decade ago, he did a movie called *Soul Plane* that tanked at the box office. It was supposed to be his *Coming to America* and it ended up being his *Going Home from Hollywood.* But Kevin took it all in stride. He rebuilt his career step by step. He wrote new material. He traveled state to state, from small comedy club to small comedy club, honing his material and sharpening his craft. Every time he stepped on a stage in front of twenty people, he was asking for and being given the opportunity to do the work. He's a big star now. I have as much respect for Kevin's journey as I do for the place he is in now.

Recently, I had the opportunity to work with Marcus Luttrell on a documentary I produced. Marcus and his brother began training to be Navy Seals at the age of fourteen. Sixteen years later, he was thirty years old and assigned to one of the most dangerous missions in the fight against the Taliban. Marcus was the only member of his team who survived. His book *Lone Survivor* was later made into a movie. Because of my dad, I have the utmost respect for the men and women who serve in our armed forces. During our work on the documentary, Marcus kept comparing his time as a Navy Seal with my time as a football player. I'll tell you the truth, it made me a little uncomfortable. I didn't feel like it was appropriate to compare the world of professional sports to the life-and-death situations this man faced as one of the most elite members of the American military. But after really talking to him and remembering what Earl taught me, I got it.

Although our training and experience were different, Marcus and I were both steeped in the art of mental toughness. It's about finding the focus and confidence to attack whatever challenge arises with everything you've got and then some. Earl Leggett taught me how to find that "then some" when I thought my tank was completely empty.

We've all got it, the ability to push ourselves to the next level—whatever the next level might be—but not all of us are accessing it. Marcus has a phrase that I just love. He likes to say, "That juice is worth the squeeze." When we push ourselves, sometimes it hurts. But when you acknowledge that you've got more to give, you put yourself in the position of getting more. A little less sleep. A little harder workout. A little more time preparing and studying for whatever you want to excel at instead of zoning out after work when you just want to collapse on the couch. All of it is worth it because it gets you that much closer to your dreams. Earl used to have a sign in his office that read, "What did you do to get better today?" For me, that just about sums it up.

7

FATHERHOOD (OR, THANKS, DAD, FOR SETTING THE BAR SO HIGH)

Rule #7

Ask yourself, "Am I the man or the woman that I hoped to be?"
If you want to *be* more, then you've got to *do* more.

T HREE YEARS INTO my career as a Giant, Wanda became pregnant with our second child. I was over the moon. For the better part of a year, I was able to watch up close as my wife's body developed and changed. During the day, my job was to take players down, to "stomp you out." At night, when I came home to my wife, there was nothing I could do but sit back and marvel at the miracle her body was making.

We followed one of those week-by-week journals, and after I'd put Tanita, who was three, and prime for bedtime stories and tick-les, to bed, we'd talk about what was happening with the baby. Week four, the baby is the size of a poppy seed. Week five, the baby is the size of a tadpole. By week ten, the baby has working arm joints; cartilage and bone are forming; she or he is starting to swallow and kick. Every week, another development. Every doctor visit was a moment to pause and thank God that so far, so good. Both baby and mama were healthy and fine.

I had been away at school when my daughter was born, so when Wanda went into labor it was all brand-new for me. As a profes-sional athlete, you put your body through punishing levels of pain. But to watch a mother give birth is a mind-blowing experience. Just the Sunday before, I'd been crushed in a tackle. Five guys, all 285 pounds plus, came crashing down on me. The crush of that tackle was nothing compared to the knock-me-over-with-a-feather woo-ziness I felt when they handed me Michael Junior and I felt his tiny head rest against my chest. I knew, once again, what people meant when they said the moment you become a parent, you have agreed forever to walk around with your heart outside of your body.

I was twenty-three years old, and I had been a parent longer than I'd had a full-time job. Wanda was twenty-one. In football, you go to practice, you watch the film, and you study the playbooks. Along with your coaches, you analyze the threats and you prepare for every scenario you can think of. I wanted to handle my marriage and par-enthood the same way. We brought Michael Junior home from the hospital, and as I drove the car, a thousand scenarios ran through my head. How can I be a better father? How can I be a better hus-band? How can I make it so that this kid has everything and really knows me, the way I know my dad? I remembered how hurt I was when I discovered the "Booty on Back" nickname and how my dad helped me lose the weight that made me a chubby kid, and how, in the process, I'd discovered so much courage and confidence that it took me all the way to the NFL. Michael Junior was just three days old, but I was already thinking it through: how we might work out together, how to teach him about diet and fitness, how to carve out the time in the off-season to take him on fishing trips, the way my dad took me.

We arrived at our home, and I helped Wanda into bed so she could rest. I put Michael Junior in his crib, looked in his eyes, and thought, "Who are you going to be?" And my second thought was "I don't want to screw this up."

When you come into the NFL, you're naïve. Ostensibly, you're a professional, but at heart football is still a game. Every day, no matter how hard the workouts, no matter how punishing the competition, you're playing the game you love. I remember thinking, "Man, they give me money for this now? I didn't get this paycheck at college." You realize it's a business when you see guys you were drafted with start to disappear. The guy who was your buddy last year? He's not here this year. You don't know how he's feeding his family. The pressure can motivate you because you think, "If I don't make this my business, then how am I going to take care of myself?" Your entire focus shifts when you ask yourself, "If this goes away, how am I going to support not only myself but also my family?"

It may have been the inspiration of becoming a father for the second time, or it may have been that, three years into my tenure with the Giants, I was coming into my own, but after Michael Junior was born, my football career began to take off. I racked up a career high of fourteen sacks in the season; I was invited to my first Pro Bowl and the Associated Press named me to the First-Team All Pro for the very first time. It felt good.

The Pro Bowl—the once-a-year all-star game that pits the most accomplished players of the year against each other—was an especially nice prize. Every year, the NFL's best players are invited to play for a week in Hawaii. It's a sweet deal: all the fun of the game, a chance to play with all of these guys that you compete against all season. You've played together in the cold, the rain, and the snow. Then you all get to go to Hawaii where the dome is called—get this—the Aloha Stadium. Sure, there's some prize money on the line, but the emphasis is on having fun. My first Pro Bowl reminded me of what it felt like to be a kid again, a feeling I hadn't had in a really long time.

All the sunshine in Hawaii, however, couldn't mask the fact that a dark storm was brewing at home. My marriage wasn't working, and though we were both trying hard to make a success out of it, I know that for me, divorce felt like failure. So we kept at it, but there came a point when we sat down and were able to look at each other and realize that we had come together with all the energy and euphoria of teenagers. When we stopped fussing and arguing, when I stopped being mad, I could close my eyes and remember what it was like after Wanda and I had our first kiss. It was like we had entered a bubble. There was nobody else in the world but us. Nothing and no one else existed or mattered. But it had been almost ten years since that first kiss, that first crazy wave of puppy love. When I was in college in Houston and she was back home in Germany, we had made the wave last. The wave had brought us two children; it had given me the family and the foundation upon which I'd built my professional football career. But when it was just the two of us, there was little of that passion, little of that love. Couples adapt. Love morphs. But what we wanted to do, more than anything, was to step away from the memory of our teenage selves and see who we might become if we gave each other the chance to be free and grow up. Wanda and I decided that while we would no longer be married, we would always be family.

My parents still lived in Mannheim, and my three older brothers worked for my dad in his transport business. Wanda made the decision to move back to Germany. She wanted to be closer to her family and to my family. I didn't want her to go. I didn't want to be so far away from my kids. But I also knew how much I had loved growing up in Germany. As usual, I could see that Wanda was thinking about the kids first and foremost. They would have an amazing quality of life in Germany.

The moment their plane took off from Newark Airport, I felt a rush of sadness. Tanita was only five years old. Michael Junior was only two. Wanda, who had been the love of my life since I was seventeen years old, was gone. I had accomplished so much over the past few years: college all-star, and I not only made it to the pros but was defensive end for one of the most iconic teams in the NFL: the New York Giants. But sitting in my bedroom, alone and far away from my children, my parents, my brothers, I felt like I'd hardly made any progress at all. I'd swapped one sad square box—my dorm room at Texas Southern—for another, the bedroom in my new apartment in New Jersey.

I reminded myself that Michael Junior and Tanita were all the more reason I needed to work harder and play harder on the gridiron, six days a week. Football made it possible to give both my parents and my children a better life. But it was hard. I didn't get to see my family and they didn't get to come out and see me play. My parents never saw me play in high school. My dad never saw me play in college, except on tape. I tried to be stoic, tried to play like it wasn't getting to me. But every morning, when I woke up in an empty house, the distance was like a crowbar prying open my chest. Everyone I loved, everyone I called family, lived an ocean away.

My own father had been such a hands-on dad. He had shaped my mind, my character, and my spirit with his daily interactions. It gave me some comfort to know that he was still young enough to play an active role in my kids' upbringing. I wanted to be there. I wanted to be more than a means of support. I was a twenty-five-year-old football player with an NFL contract. I did what I could, but when I sat quietly with myself and asked, "Am I the man, the father, that I hoped to be?" I judged myself lacking. I wanted to do and be more.

Around this time, one series of events filled me with pride rather than doubt. One day, I got the call that makes every mama's boy football player grin ear to ear. Did I want to be in a Campbell's Soup commercial with my mom? I thought she'd say yes. But I wanted to make sure before I accepted.

I said, "Mom, they want to know if you want to be in a soup commercial."

She said, "Sure. Yeah."

I teased her a little and said, "But, Mom, you can't act."

She said, "Boy, what have I been doing all of my life? I've been acting every day for years."

I said, "Really, Mom?"

She said, "Uh-huh. Acting like having six kids wasn't driving me crazy. Bring it on."

It was great. They flew my mother to New York, put her up at a fancy hotel, and gave her her very own Glam Squad, with a hairstylist and makeup. They even sent a fancy Town Car to pick her up and bring her to the set. That's the kind of thing that makes you feel so proud and happy. I can shower my mom with love and presents all day and all night long. But when someone else does it, when someone else gives her that extra special treatment, it's icing on the cake.

I was so happy to be on set with my mom. So happy to be filming a commercial for a brand I actually remember loving as a kid. Even on those American bases, especially on those American bases, you could find Campbell's soup. It felt like, in some small way, we were living out the American dream. Then the camera came on. My mother froze. She sputtered her lines like she was Jaws in a James Bond movie.

"You. Need. A. Hot. Bowl . . . Of Chunky Soup . . . To . . . Fill . . . You . . . Up . . ."

Take 2. Take 3. Take 10.

I turned to her and said, "What are you doing, expert? You're supposed to know this!"

Initially a little wooden, once she relaxed, she was great. We ended up shooting even more commercials. On the New York City subway. In Central Park. Campbell's Soup turned my mother into a celebrity, which made her happy, which made her baby son happy.

I don't know if this is a Strahan Rule or one of those rules that's as true in one culture as it is in another, a universal truth: If Mom is happy, the whole family is happy.

8

WHY PLAY *SHOULD* BE THE WORK OF ADULTS

Rule #8

Play is the business of adults. Plato said, "You can discover more about a person in an hour of play than in a year of conversation."

THE TERM "QUARTERBACK SACK" is credited to a Hall of Fame defensive player named Deacon Jones who first began to use the term in the 1960s, a decade before I was born. Jones was born in Eatonville, the same segregated Florida town that gave the world Zora Neale Hurston, whose tales of Southern men who loved hard and the women who loved harder became a cornerstone of American literature. From the beginning, racial discrimination was a huge force for him. The youngest of eight children, he played high school football, baseball, and basketball. At the age of fourteen, Jones recalled seeing a car full of white teenagers hit an elderly black woman from his local church in the head with a giant watermelon. The teens drove away laughing, but a few days later the woman died from the injuries. Jones won a football scholarship to South Carolina State, but the scholarship was revoked when the school learned that he had participated in civil rights protests. He transferred to Mississippi Vocational, where, as part of the traveling team, he and other black teammates would have to sleep on cots in the opposing team's gym because no local motels would rent them a room. Jones would later say, "Thank God I had the ability to play a violent game like football. It gave me an outlet for the anger in my heart."

Jones began to use the term "sack" because by stopping the quarterback (or another offensive passer), the defense devastates the play in much the same way that great historic battles like the Sack of Rome devastated the ancient cities. I was lucky enough to get to know Deacon before he passed away. He took care of me. Long before I had established my reputation in the league, he made a point of seeking me—a second round draft pick who had yet to earn his stripes—out. He'd not only watch me play but also encourage me to keep at it. His attention legitimized me in many ways and gave me a reason to push harder. His stories were legendary and had a way of inspiring me throughout my career.

When I was a player, sacks were my specialty. I did what I could to give myself the physical advantage to be an outstanding player. The average NFL player plays for just three seasons. I was on year seven of what I hoped would be a decade-plus career. In the weight room, I didn't lift weights just on the days when all the other linemen lifted. I lifted on the days the backs and receivers lifted too, maybe just a little something for my neck and shoulders. On another scheduled day off, I alternated sit-ups and other core exercises with weight training for my legs. Just as my father had done all that research to create weight training programs for me when I was a chubby kid in Germany trying to lose weight, I worked with the team trainers to fine-tune my work so that I could push my body harder, but still stay injury free. Finding the little ways to stay ahead has always been important to me.

The physical training paid off. In 1999, I had fifteen game-changing sacks, and my new contract reflected my value to the team. Then my sack total dropped to five and a half, and the sports critics—both in New York and nationally—noticed. I took it hard. Noticing my funk, Jessie Armstead, one of my best friends on the team, urged me to stop worrying about the record. He said, "Let the sack stat go and just play." At the time, I won't lie: the criticism stung. But I've been so fortunate to have good people around me give me sound advice. Jessie was right. I had trained my body; I had reviewed the tapes and studied the skills of my various opponents. Now it was time to play for the fun of it. It didn't happen overnight. There was a learning curve involved; that is, I had to learn how to let go. But once I began to play in the moment, to really connect with the other members of my team and not just pursue sacks for the sake of sack glory, a funny thing happened: my game improved. My mental game had finally caught up with my physical game.

It's a kind of irony that any professional athlete realizes sooner rather than later: we "play" sports, but when you are fortunate to make your living as an athlete, there comes a point where the fun part of it all can go out the window. But reconnecting to play is fundamental to success, no matter what you do for a living. Scientists have found that play is directly related to huge health benefits, including lower stress levels, as well as better memory retention and a stronger sense of teamwork, which can all translate directly into greater success. Interestingly, playing video games at your desk when you're supposed to be working on that year-end report won't do the trick. The most productive play is off-line and involves other people, be it playing foosball during your lunch hour or even just joking around with your coworkers before a meeting starts. Albert Einstein said that "play is the highest form of research."

During the years when I was chasing a sack record on the football field and learning to let go, to play—all the while achieving more professionally than I had dreamed—I had fun cracking jokes on various people around the team, including the stretch coach, Jerry Palmieri. Jerry drove this beat-up old Econovan. At Giants Stadium, we'd had a series of break-ins while we were in practice; someone was breaking into cars and stealing stuff. The team finally got better security for the parking lot and the break-ins stopped.

One day, I walked up to our coach and said, "Excuse me, Coach."

He said, "Yes?"

I said, "We had another parking lot incident."

You could just see him hanging his head, like "Oh no, not again."

I said, "Somebody actually broke into Jerry's car and installed a heater and a stereo system."

The whole team cracked up.

Another time, we were at practice and we heard what sounded like a gunshot. All the guys jumped up and looked around, asking,

"What was that?" We had been at practice for about an hour. I said, "Oh that? That's just Jerry's car finally shutting off."

But nobody brought the comedy like my friend Jay Glazer. We were both just out of school and we were both making our way. Jay, in the early years of our friendship, was making no money at all and didn't have a car. He could barely afford bus fare from the city to Giants Stadium every day, so every day I drove him into Manhattan from the stadium, which was about ten and a half miles away.

You'd think that since I was the one with the NFL contract, Jay would be dripping with gratitude for those rides. But that's not the way Jay Glazer operates, and I love that about him. He treats every guy as his equal. Ask him what he thought about me when he first met me, and he won't give me any props for being the Giants' first-draft pick the year I was signed or the college sack king who came to the big city with the skills to pay the bills. Jay will tell you, "I just thought he was a big, goofy guy with a gap in his teeth and a speech impediment." Thanks a lot, Jay.

My star began to rise on the Giants, but Jay didn't care. I was his friend and I was his ride and he made sure that I kept to it. Sometimes I would be late coming out of practice because I'd be getting a treatment or some sort of physical therapy for an injury. Jay would start banging on the door. "Come on, Stray! Gotta go, gotta go. I need that ride. I've got a hot date tonight."

For *years,* I drove Jay Glazer back into the city after my practice. You would have thought I was his chauffeur, not a professional athlete. But those car rides were an invaluable time. We laughed and joked, but we also opened up to each other: building the core of our friendship and planning our biggest dreams. Jay saw a career for me in broadcast way back when other people thought I was just a big lunky football player with a Texas, by way of Germany, accent. And I knew that Jay would be a star in broadcast sports journalism because his passion for the game, matched with his ability to scoop a news story, was unparalleled. Now that he is that big TV star, I joke that he should write me a nice big check for all those rides I gave him when he didn't even have bus fare. The way I see it, Jay Glazer owes me about twenty-two thousand dollars in gas and Lincoln Tunnel tolls. But that's not why we're still friends. Our friendship has lasted until this day because he makes me laugh. He's one of the many people in my life with whom I can indulge the playful side of my personality. If you don't have someone like that in your corner, your team is incomplete.

THE POWER OF ROUTINES

Rule #9

Not if but when. The secret to success lies not in luck but in the things you do every day.

DON'T LIMIT MYSELF, and I tell my kids, "Don't let anyone limit you." It's one of the great things I learned from my dad. The word "if" was not part of his vocabulary; it was always "when." My father never said, "If you get a college scholarship . . ." or "If you get drafted by the pros . . ." It was *always* when. "When you get a scholarship . . ." "When you get drafted by the pros . . ." Just by the words he chose, he made it seem like these things were supposed to happen.

But we all know that positive self-talk will get you only so far. For me, the power of routine has always been the strongest bridge between "if" and "when." *The Happiness Project* writer Gretchen Rubin has said that one of her secrets of adulthood is that "what

you do every day matters more than what you do once in a while."
Long before I ever picked up a football, my parents instilled in us
the importance of routines. You get up and you say, "Good morning" every day; you don't just grumble to your folks on the way to
brushing your teeth. You make your bed every day. You eat a healthy
breakfast every day. Just as our parents never called in sick to work,
we were expected to do our jobs—our homework first, household
chores second—without exception.

Forming new habits can be hard, but this is the thing about routines: once you learn them, they make life easier. Sports psychologist Sean McCann echoes a lot of what I learned as an athlete: "Some
psychologists believe that over 90% of our behaviors are automatic
habits or learned, unconscious behaviors . . . Routines that take care
of the little things, free up brain space to focus on the things that
really matter."

That was certainly true of me on game day. The earlier I could
be, the more in control I felt. As a player, I learned that arriving on
time for a game wasn't good enough. When I would go into the
locker room, get dressed, and then a short time later pop out when
we had to stretch as a team before playing the game, I just did not
play well. I did not feel well. So I made a habit of getting to the game
two and a half hours early. If I was going to be thrown into this
game, expected to perform as a gladiator, then I wanted to get to
know the stage well before my entrance.

Home game or away, I used the same routine to transform my
mind before the game, to gather my strength: I would stand in
the tunnel alone, hours before the game began. I'd start out by
listening to R&B, artists like Alicia Keys, Dave Hollister, Mary J.
Blige, and Keith Sweat. I'd take my time and slowly walk out onto

the field. Everybody thought I was listening to gangster rap, but it was mellow R&B, mood music with which I could take it all in, getting the feel of the environment so that when I did come out officially, it wasn't overwhelming. If I just ran out there, minutes before the game, with the rest of the team, it would almost feel as if the environment were an additional opponent. But when I took the time to walk out on the field early, I could soak it all in and appreciate the hallowed and glorious tradition of which we were a part.

That was my calm. Then I'd go back to the locker room and change the music, change the mood. I'd up the tempo with some hip-hop and begin the steps, both physical and mental, that would get me ready for the game. It turns out that researchers have long believed that music has the power to reduce stress, increase focus, and bring more productivity to the task at hand. Elena Mannes, author of *The Power of Music: Pioneering Discoveries in the New Science of Song,* discovered that "listening to music stimulates more parts of the brain than any other human function."

Scientists agree that music can help lower blood pressure, reduce cardiac complications, and increase our immunity. We know that music makes us feel good, and that's because listening to an artist we love ups the flow of dopamine, the chemical that makes us feel pleasure. But music is one of the greatest tools we have in fighting the symptoms of our overbooked and overscheduled lives. A great playlist can give us the thing that we all crave: more energy. Nearly a century before spin classes became all the rage, according to an article in *Scientific American*, in 1911, American investigator Leonard Ayres discovered that cyclists pedaled faster while a band was playing than when it was silent. It's not just the bass line of a great song that drives us to move faster. It turns out that at the first sign of fatigue our brain starts sending the message that we are tired, so tired. Music literally drowns out those messages of exhaustion so that we don't hear them and therefore aren't affected by them.

I *still* use music to set the tone for my day. The first thing I do when I wake up in the morning is listen to music. It's the key to starting my day off right. The truth is that I'm a pretty happy guy now. And my morning music ritual today, as it was when I played professional football, is one of the keys to making sure that each day is as good as it can possibly be.

I wish I could say that I hop out of bed before the alarm goes off, ready and roaring to embrace the day, that I automatically wake up happy. That would be a lie. I'm not a lark. Like most Americans, I tend to stay up too late and sleep too little, so when the first alarm goes off—I hit snooze a few times until, moved by the music, I roll over with a smile on my face. By the third alarm, my bedroom is starting to resemble the set of *LIVE with Kelly and Michael:* the music is bumping, I'm raring to go, and the day has started.

Studies have shown that by the time we hit the bed at night, the average American will have made thirty-five thousand decisions that day. Our daily decisions range from the small—what will I have for breakfast? should I wear the blue shirt or the gray one?—to the medium—should I stop at Starbucks on the way to work? will I go to the gym at lunchtime?—to the more consequential—should I ask that girl out on a date? should I ask my boss for a raise? Will interest rates decline further or should I go ahead and buy that new house?

I've found, again and again, that when I start my day with music—when I take the time to set my alarm not to blare like a fire alarm, but to wake me up with the music that I love—I'm far more likely to feel in control and more optimistic about the day ahead. It's not that Bill Withers singing "Lovely Day," which is one of the songs I set the alarm to, means that I'm not going to get caught in traffic, or someone's not going to call me with unfortunate news, or I'm not going to have to work a twelve-hour day. But the right song, first thing in the morning, has a halo effect on the day. It's so simple. Absolutely something that anyone can do.

The thing that's so genius about music is that it makes you move. How you move affects your mood. It's hard to feel lethargic when you're jumping up and down. It's hard to stay in a bad mood when you're grooving to a banging beat. When I played football, I began every Sunday with what became known as my "Stomp You Out" pep talk. I would get so excited in the middle of the huddle that I would just jump up, come down, and stomp. What I saw very quickly is that my excitement was contagious. The other guys would get excited too.

Unfortunately (or fortunately), we don't begin every day in a huddle with our best friends and favorite family members cheering us on to have an awesome day. But we can choose the words we begin our day with, the music and the movements. We can give ourselves that little five-minute pause where we get excited to stomp out whatever we need to do today.

Reading is also an important part of my early morning routine. I always read a few paragraphs of an inspiring book before I get out of bed. Currently, it's a book called *Journey to the Heart*. My friend LG gave it to me, and like the music, it sets the tone for my day. I think about my brain the same way I think about my body: You put junk in, you get junky results. You put something positive in and you get a better result. Today's quote read:

The mind is connected to the heart. Value the power of clear, conscious thought. Value your mind and its power by valuing the wisdom and power of an open heart.

I'll be thinking about that quote throughout the day: when I'm walking to work and someone stops me to take a photo and my first thought is "I can't be late to work," I'll think about that quote and remember that taking a photo with someone who is kind enough to be a fan of the show is one way to keep an open heart. I'll think about the quote when we have a guest who is a little reserved, and I have to challenge myself to stay in the moment and keep asking questions, instead of thinking ahead to the next guest and the rest of my day. And I'll think about the quote when my daughter Sophia calls me unexpectedly and I'm so happy to hear from her that time literally stops and there's nowhere else I'd rather be and nothing else I'd rather do than talk to her. Then after our phone call, I'll feel how I'm energized—like I just had two cups of coffee—and how I'm ready and happy, clear and conscious—to attack the rest of my day.

Reading my daily quote grounds me. Then it's back to my music, my "Happiness" playlist. I start getting ready for work and I'm grooving to a favorite song, I may be singing along to the lyrics, but what I'm thinking is this: another day, another chance. Another chance to do good work, to connect with amazing people, to spend time with the friends and family that I love. If that's not a reason to wake up happy, then I don't know what is.

That's how I start each day. Then at the end of the day, I take a few minutes to review: What did I do well? What could I have done better? When I played football, I spent hours reviewing the game film of both my own team and the teams we competed against.

Studying the film helped me improve the things that were good and adjust the parts of my game that needed work. In broadcast, I review the notes from our producers: both from that day's show and for the upcoming show.

Dr. Joseph Cardillo is not only a lifelong Giants fan but also an expert on positive thinking. In his last book on the subject, *Body Intelligence: Harness Your Body's Energies for Your Best Life,* Dr. Cardillo suggests that for a restful evening, start with rebooting your commute: "Music is a great way to make the energy shift from work to home. So some good vibrations on your drive home works wonders. Decide on the type or mindset you want to take home and the energy you want to be feeling (more alert or more relaxed) and create a playlist that will deliver. Use scent. How about the cologne your husband wore on your first date or the perfume your wife wore? Scent is faster than any other sensory detail and will bypass—as music does—your thinking brain and powerfully influence your emotions."

Here are Dr. Cardillo's top four tips for creating a restorative evening routine:

- **Slow down dinnertime.** "Have a relaxed dinner with no electronics around. Mindfulness helps. Taking a slow breath and the time to slow down, consider the good food you are about to eat and, if you are with others, the goodness of having them in this moment as part of your life, particularly loved ones, helps plug energy drains and increase your positive energy."

- **Talk it out.** "Have good conversation. Work the solutions and don't spin your wheels in the problem. Or just let yourself know that there is a solution out there and stop with that. Sometimes—often—that's the first step to seeing a solution. To that same end, it's refreshing and strengthening to talk about dreams and listen to the dreams of others, especially at night. This makes you feel good and allows your unconscious mind to give your conscious, analytical mind a break and creatively delve into ways of achieving those dreams for you without your even knowing it is working for you and without stressing out your conscious mind."

- **Read something inspiring.** "Just before bedtime read something philosophical or spiritual that nurtures your spirit—by spiritual I don't necessarily mean denominational. What's important is that it makes you feel good and suggests how you can live an even more spiritual life."

- **Meditate.** "Lastly, meditate to feel your energetic connection to yourself and beyond to all of life. Start by slowing down and deepening your breathing. Breathe as if filling your lungs from bottom up. Repeat the words 'I am here' as you breathe in and 'Here is now' as you exhale. You can say these silently in your mind. You can also make up your own phrases that will place you into the present moment.

  "Next, place your hand on your heart and feel its rhythm. When we were in the womb, we luxuriated in the safe comfort of our mother's heartbeat. These beats are ingrained in you from the first cells that made you, you. By mindfully placing your attention on your own heartbeat, you can feel some of the safety and comfort of this primal musical memory and use it to help relax.

"Finally, extend your awareness outward beyond your body. Move it through all material things in your environment, outward toward the stars, through the stars, all the space between and beyond them, past the last light, past the last dark. Hold that mindset for a while. With practice you will be able to hold it longer. Then slowly retrace your path backward to where you began. This type of meditation practiced before bedtime will help you relieve any lingering anxieties and help send you off into dreamland."

I'm not trying to sell my routine or even Dr. Cardillo's routines to you. But I am encouraging you in your quest for happiness, or transformation, to find your own routines so that you can free up more creative, energetic space in your own mind and perform better under pressure—another benefit, the science tells us, of the power of routines. It's important to plan routines for both your high-energy bursts of the day—working out, accomplishing the biggest things on your to-do list at work and at home—as well as the more relaxed parts of your day—dinnertime with family or friends, a mindful, quiet lunch, a midday walk, or your evening wind-down. Don't just rush from task to task; utilize the power of the pause. Literally take a deep breath when you finish one activity and are transitioning into the next—this will help you be in the moment and tap into the energy you need for whatever you're doing next. I need one kind of energy for my early morning workouts with my trainer, Latreal Mitchell, and a different energy entirely right before Kelly and I walk onto the *LIVE* stage. My downtime energy varies too. When I pause, I can appreciate a Saturday afternoon watching my girls compete in horseback riding and be totally in the moment when I meet my friends at the cigar bar for a night out on the town. The pause is almost like looking at one of those maps in the mall. You know when you look at the map and you find the button that says, "You are here"? That feeling of relief you get when you know exactly where you are and where you're going to next. We can all tap into that if we take the time to pause between tasks.

10

MAKING IT RIGHT

Rule #10

Though it's hard to appreciate this when you're going through a painful passage, it's the bad experiences that often teach you the most.

FTER A FEW YEARS, both Wanda and I remarried again. My second marriage didn't work out, and I'm sad to say that you probably know—or can Google—more than I ever wanted to share about how we split up and what went wrong. It's hard when your personal life becomes tabloid fodder. What makes me sad is that my daughters will someday be able to find a lot of that garbage online.

One of the things I can say with confidence is that the divorce was the worst thing that ever happened to me. But in many ways it taught me one of my most important lessons. Ending that marriage taught me that I had to find myself, personally. That's not any fault of my ex-wife's at all.

Jean was a very strong woman, and because I had married so young the first time around, I wanted to be with someone who seemed ready to be in charge. But as many people, men and women, have learned, you can lose yourself in someone else to the point where it's not healthy. I began living her life, not my own, and her life made little room for the people who were important to me—namely my parents, my children, and my friends—which kind of made me go, "Okay. I don't think this is going to change or get any better."

It dawned on me: I had to take control because one day I was going to wake up and say, "I've never had my family around to enjoy the success that I've had as an athlete. If I separate myself from the people I love to preserve this marriage, then the day will surely come when I don't have this relationship and it'll be too late to get back all that I've sacrificed along the way." All of the people I was shutting out—my parents, my misfit band of friends, even my first wife, Wanda—had been there to support me from the beginning. I grew up emotionally in that divorce because I learned the hard way that true love should *multiply* the joy in your life, not diminish all the love you already have and have treasured for years. If your partner in life doesn't do that—multiply your joy—you're probably not in the right relationship. (I have more to say about love in the epilogue.)

Having to work through a failed relationship while raising children is like getting a master's degree in partnership skills. Some people say that I have two failed marriages. I'd rather say that I have two master's degrees in human relationships. One day I'll get that PhD, and hopefully it will last forever. Our twin daughters, Sophia and Isabella, were just four months old when Jean and I split. I had made what I'd decided was a mistake the first time around with Michael Junior and Tanita. By letting them move back to Germany,

I had robbed them of my presence and I had robbed myself of the opportunity to be in their life on a day-to-day basis. Without wanting to, I'd become a special-occasion dad.

When Jean was pregnant with the twins, I'd read a number of articles that said the first three years are significant in terms of bonding between children and their fathers. On the other hand, the research shows that for all sorts of biological reasons, mothers and children share a bond from birth. The mother is usually the nurturer, the caregiver. It's different with fathers; it takes years for that bond to truly develop and cement. I went to court and insisted that I be granted joint custody of the girls in order to establish that bond, which meant that Jean couldn't take them out of New York State since my work was here, playing for the Giants.

I think the judge thought I was some sort of self-entitled pro athlete who was trying to run a power game on my soon-to-be ex-wife. So the judge gave me a test. He said, "For the first six months, you have to take the girls every other day. If I find out that a nanny or some other professional is caring for the children when you're not at work, then I will grant full custody to Jean and she can move wherever she likes."

I gave that judge my best Bernie Mac grin and let him know "I ain't scared." But, truthfully, I was. At the time, I was renting a townhouse from one of my old teammates, Keith "the Hammer" Hamilton. I drove over to the nearest Target and stocked up on everything that I might need: diapers, wipes, formula, undershirts, onesies, nontoxic laundry detergent, burp cloths, two infant tubs, a baby thermometer, and two giant Diaper Genies with some of those citrus deodorizing disks. I had already set up a room with two cribs, and my ride was already stocked with two baby car seats. I was ready to be Mr. Mom.

That first day, I had a tape of Donovan McNabb to watch, and
I did so with a baby on each arm. You spill a lot of actual blood and
guts on that football field, but I have to say the amount of saliva,
poop, and throw-up that I saw with the twins could give a grown
man the chills. But something else kicks in around four months
out; just when you think you can't change another messy diaper or
warm up another bottle in the middle of the night, the baby starts
to smile. I would lay Sophia and Isabella in the Pack 'n Play as I
studied my playbook and went over film, and when I looked over,
they'd gurgle and grin at me. As a guy who was used to hearing
eighty thousand fans cheer for him on a Sunday afternoon, I found
it amazing that a smile from two little baby girls could lay me out
flat. Before they could even talk, we had our "just us" moments,
like when I was juggling work and warming up food at the same
time my parents would call from Texas because they had heard
some foolishness about my divorce on television. I would look over
at Sophia and Isabella. One of them would meet my eye and give
me a little smile, like "We see you trying. You got this." It was all the
encouragement I needed.

In the locker room, I'd hear amazing stories about what the guys
had done the night before. Nope, I wasn't getting bottle service at
the latest clubs. I wasn't on a boat, riding around New York Harbor
with this rapper or that producer. And sadly, I wasn't backstage at
the Victoria's Secret fashion show, hanging out with those Angels.
But it didn't bother me because I was enjoying my here and now.

All I could think about was that judge. If I hired a sitter and some
photo of me partying showed up in the paper, then it would've been
over. He would've said, "You don't want to be a father and you're
not going to have joint custody of those kids." Given what I had

learned from my experiences with my first two children, parenting them from afar, I wanted to be more involved.

I have close friends whose parents divorced when they were young. I remember them saying to me, "Michael, as much hell as you're getting out of this, why don't you just remove yourself from the situation? Your kids will understand." I think if I hadn't had Michael and Tanita, I could have done it. I would have said, "To hell with this. I'll catch them when they get older. This is crazy." That path wasn't for me. I refused to give up. "It is on," I thought. For three years, we'll build this relationship. No matter what, these girls will know their dad.

I had spent a lot of the year that the girls were born injured with a torn pectoral muscle. The next year, 2005, I rebounded with a fury, racking up double-digit sacks. It was an amazing year in my career, but when I close my eyes and play back the memories, Sophia and Isabella almost crowd all the football out. There was the first time Isabella laughed, and when they started playing patty-cake and peekaboo. There was the first time Sophia raised her head and chest when she was on her stomach, just checking out the world like a little bitty Sphinx. I remember when both girls started to crawl, and when they started to crawl with *speed,* the way they scurried across the hardwood floors like little bumper cars. I remember when Sophia stood up for the first time and how hard she laughed when she fell right back down. Isabella was the first to call me Da-Da; Sophia followed her pretty quickly. For a while, they both just said it for the sake of saying it, and it was almost like a song: "Da-da-da . . . Da-da-da . . . Da-da . . . Da-da . . . Da-da-da."

When the girls started eating real food, the kitchen would look like a whole class of fifth graders had been in my house playing paintball. But instead of using paint pellets, they'd used Gerber baby peas and carrots, beets and sweet potato. Those girls tore up that townhouse and nearly tore me up in the process too. But I achieved my goal. I wasn't the dad who swung by on Sunday afternoons, every other week. I wasn't just the guy who signed the child support check and sent a ton of presents on Christmas and birthdays. I was Dad, and they lived with me every other day in our house that we shared.

Anyone who has twins knows that while they are double the fun, they are also double the work. Some of the most precious moments to me were when the girls would wear themselves out and finally fall asleep. I marveled at their sleeping faces. Even before they could charm me with their humor or bowl me over with their sass, I was like putty in their little hands. I'd stand over their crib and wonder how I could protect them from everything, make smooth every step that they might take. One would think I would hit the pillow the moment they fell asleep. Instead, I would stay awake and watch them because it was the sweetest thing. It was like the Aerosmith song:

> *I could stay awake just to hear you breathing*
> *Watch you smile while you are sleeping*
> *While you're far away dreaming*
> *I could spend my life in this sweet surrender*
> *I could stay lost in this moment forever*
> *Every moment spent with you is a moment I treasure*
>
> *Don't want to close my eyes*
> *I don't want to fall asleep*

'Cause I'd miss you baby
And I don't want to miss a thing
'Cause even when I dream of you
The sweetest dream will never do
I'd still miss you baby
And I don't want to miss a thing

All the effort I put into being there for them those first three years had an unexpected effect on my relationship with my older children. I realized I couldn't be the man I wanted to be with Sophia and Isabella if I wasn't a good father to Tanita and Michael Junior. It was impossible. It was just in my heart: I had to be a better father all the way around, including for Dorian, Wanda's son from another marriage and Tanita and Michael Junior's half brother. I treat him and take care of him as if he were my son because it's very important to me that Michael Junior and Tanita have the confidence of knowing that their mother is fine, their brother is fine, everybody is well taken care of. It would be hypocritical to be in court saying I want to be a great father to these twins when I wasn't doing the same for my other children. I began to make more of an effort so that there were special things that I did with just Michael Junior and Tanita. And while I started out making a conscientious effort to make amends, I learned what we all learn: You give what you yourself need. I needed that time with the kids as much if not more then they needed me. When I'm with my kids, the older ones or the twins, I'm at my happiest, nothing else matters.

11

WHAT I LEARNED FROM CHRIS MARTIN AND COLDPLAY

Rule #11

You can't change other people, but you can change how you are around them, and sometimes, a lot of times, that's more than enough.

M Y BATTLE WITH Giants coach Tom Coughlin was, and in some quarters still is, legendary, but what it taught me is applicable to anyone who's had what they believe is a horrible boss. This is the thing: I truly believe that although the archetype of the difficult boss is hilarious on film, the truly horrible boss is a myth. There are talented people who don't know how to communicate with and inspire the people they lead (which, to my mind, is the category that Tom fell into). Then there are people who are out of their depth, and so they compensate in all kinds of ways. And behind door number three of bad bosses, we have the people who never really grew up. One study of US employees who consider their bosses to be a nightmare compared their "leader" to a tyrannical toddler: selfish, overdemanding, impulsive, and interrupting.

None of these people are *fun* to work for, but I can tell you—from experience—that you can learn something from each kind. In particular, you'll learn something about yourself from each type that will help elevate your game, no matter what your field, and you'll learn something about human nature, which will help you in future relationships. As much as we like to think we're all these super-unique individuals, human behavior has patterns that connect us and show up time and time again. What you learn from a horrible boss could save your next relationship, or help you get along with your annoying sister, or help you win over the condo board president who likes to throw her or his weight around or the contractor who knows bupkes about time management. It's all grist for the mill. Nothing is wasted if you're paying attention and intent on improving the situation. Of course, I learned all of this the hard way.

The first time I ever met Tom Coughlin face-to-face was in his first season as head coach for the Giants. In this encounter, Tom's attitude seemed to be "You've had a pretty good career, but if you listen to every single thing I say, I'll make you a real football player." I'd heard about Tom before that meeting. At least ten players who had played for him in the past talked to me about Coughlin. Nine out of the ten complained about his unusual rules and rigidity. One player called him an abusive warden.

As I've written elsewhere, I was scheduled to be out of town for the first meeting that Coughlin called and he was furious about it. He said, "Give me the names and numbers of the people running this event and I will call them personally and cancel for you." Mind you, he never asked me if I could reschedule the event. He ordered me to do it.

I was already so over him, but I tried to compromise. I said, "Coach, how about this? I'll come in Monday at six A.M. to meet with you and the other coaches. I'll go through your strength-and-conditioning orientation and hear you out before you meet with the team. Then I'll fly out." Coughlin agreed.

Monday morning, when I walked into his office, there was a legal pad with one single piece of yellow paper left. The rest had been ripped out. A yellow no. 2 pencil lay on top of the pad. He said, "Michael, this pad and pencil is for you. I'm going to give you the same speech I will be giving the rest of the team when we meet later. I want you to write down key points. Then I want you to take it with you on the airplane and think about these points on your trip." My first thought was "This must be a joke." My second thought was "Are you freakin' kidding me? Is my twelfth season on the New York Giants really going to resemble fourth-grade detention?"

I couldn't pay attention to what else came afterward because I was so stunned at how infantilized I felt. After he finished his speech, I went downstairs, put the yellow sheet of paper in my locker, and left for my trip. When I returned for the second day of mini-camp, I got an earful of rules. For example, it's standard in the NFL that when you travel, you wear a suit and tie. Tom took the dress code one step further: you were forbidden to leave your hotel room or go to the lobby without wearing dress slacks, a collared shirt, and nice shoes.

Coughlin was also strict about time. If you weren't five minutes early, you were late. We learned this rule one day when we were given a test on our plays and assignments. Three players—cornerback Terry Cousin and linebacks Barrett Green and Carlos Emmons—were sitting outside the meeting room, working on their tests. The rest of the team had trickled into the room, but those three players wanted to take a few minutes to add the finishing touches to their answers. Our new head coach closed the door on them. When they tried to open the door, Coughlin exploded: "You three were out there messing around. You're late." He kicked them out of the meeting and fined them for being on time, which was not early enough.

There's a way to come down on players so it motivates them to work harder. John Fox, the former defensive coordinator for the Giants, had an uncanny ability to call you a dummy to the degree where you damn near wanted to thank him for such sensitive and constructive criticism. You could tell he was in this thing with you. Tom made us feel like he was always against us. The uproar Tom started among the players was the kind that had virtually disappeared from the league. The complaints grew louder and louder until the team came to me, asking me to talk to Coughlin and see what I could do to prevent a coup before the season started. So I met with him in his office. Not to complain about the rules that bothered me personally, but to explain how the rules, and the massive fines attached to them, were undermining the ability of the team to focus on the work at hand.

I told him, "Coach, I don't think it's right that you fine guys for showing up on time."

He assured me that if a guy arrived within the five-minute early "grace" period, he would let them in. Things only went from bad to worse.

I hated the man. When I say hate, I'm not using the word loosely. No, I mean, I absolutely hated the man. He would fine you for your socks being too low. He would fine you for your socks being too high. You'd get fined for wearing the wrong color sleeves under your practice jersey. He'd say, "If you can't follow my rules, you can count on being light in your paycheck."

A few weeks later, I arrived for our 7:30 A.M. meeting at 7:26. The door to the meeting room was already slammed closed. Two of our coaches sat outside the meeting room, and I pointed to the clock. They said they would let Coughlin know that I had arrived on time.

The next day I went to my locker to get dressed for practice. Sitting on my stool was a fine letter for five hundred dollars. When Tom fined us, the team management wrote a formal letter and put it either in our locker or on our stool. The fine was a slap in the face to every principle I believed in about teams and the bond and trust coaches and players had to have between and in one another.

On the way to the team walk-through, I asked, "Coach, can I talk to you for a minute? I got a letter on my stool for being fined, but I wasn't late."

Coughlin looked at me and said, "Yes, you were."

I sighed and tried not to lose my temper. "Coach, I wasn't late. Two of your coaches saw me."

He kept insisting, "You were late."

I shook my head. "But even if I wasn't there five minutes early, you said you'd give us a grace period."

He shrugged. "Well, Michael, in my eyes, you were still late. What do you want me to do, change my rules for you?"

I was starting to get impatient. It was like the conversation had taken a sharp turn from insane to psychotic. "No, Coach, I don't want you to change the rules for me," I said as politely as I could. "If I'm truly late, then fine me. But I wasn't late. I was four minutes early!"

Coughlin wasn't budging. "Next time, don't cut it so close." Then he added, "You're lucky. It could have been a fifteen-hundred-dollar fine."

That, ladies and gentlemen, was when my sportsmanship and Southern manners went out the window. I. Just. Lost. It. "You know what? Forget it!" I screamed. "Fine me fifteen hundred dollars next time. I'll just show up whenever I damn well feel like it. Screw it. I'll go to IHOP. I'll run a few errands. I'll show up whenever."

He stared at me in shock. "You can't talk to me like that," he sputtered.

Oh yeah? I let him know: "Yes, I can. If you don't respect me, I won't respect you. So I'll come in whenever I feel like it. Whether I'm a second late or an hour late, I'll come in whenever I want. Just fine me to the max."

I started to walk away and he started to follow me. The rest of the team was about thirty yards away from us. They saw us talking but didn't know what we were saying. They noticed, however, that my demeanor had changed. My switch had flipped.

Coughlin asked again, "I don't understand. Do you want me to change my rules for you?"

I looked at him and said, "It's not about me. The guys come to me when they have a problem. You think I'm dumb. You're dismissing me. But, Coach, you're losing this team. Do you hear that?"

That day turned out to be the turning point. Tom realized that I held a lot of sway in the locker room. I'd put a lot of years into the NFL. I'd been the defensive player of the year. I'd set the single-season sack record. Now I was putting that energy, that leadership, into letting him know that I thought his rules were silly and they were distracting us from the work at hand.

I found that the harder I pushed back, the more respect I got from Tom. I fully realize that had I not been a six-time Pro-Bowler, I couldn't have pushed back the way that I did. And he knew this wasn't a mere pissing match between a star player and the new head coach. We were both deeply committed to the well-being and the future of our team.

On the way to practice every day during that pre-season, I used to listen to a Coldplay album. As anyone who has watched the *LIVE with Kelly and Michael* show knows, music—and especially lyrics—are a big inspiration to me. In one particular song, Chris Martin sings:

Am I a part of the cure?
Or am I part of the disease?

Every day I'd ask myself, "Am I part of the cure? Or am I part of the disease?" in this whole situation. It was so much like the question my father would ask my brothers and me growing up: "Are you part of the problem or are you part of the solution?" Singing along to that song, hearing it in my head in the meeting room, helped me to be more patient with our new head coach and made me a better advocate for the players who increasingly turned to me to be the buffer between them and the coach's still very strict and demanding rules. I came to realize that I couldn't force Tom to change. In fact, you can't change anyone, but you can change how you are around them, and sometimes, a lot of times, that's more than enough. You're either part of the problem or part of the solution. I said, "I'll be part of the solution."

Once Tom and I stepped back from our incident, we were able to shift from focusing on our differences and arguments to trying to understand each other. As I got to know Tom Coughlin, I remembered a conversation I'd had with Keenan McCardell, who had played with the Buccaneers and the Chargers. Keenan told me, "Michael, the first year you have Tom Coughlin, you'll hate him. But the more you play for him, the more you'll understand him. The more you understand him, the more you'll like him."

Keenan was right. I began to understand Coughlin more, and because I did, I began to like him. His favorite movie is *Patton* with George C. Scott. In the movie, Patton says something like "My enemy is scared of me. My troops are scared of me. My own dog is afraid of me." I think Tom came into the Giants like Patton. He wanted to lead his troops to victory, and he thought fear was the way to do it. But the team responded most when Tom let us see his softer side. Once Kurt Warner, our former quarterback, went up with his kids in tow to see the quarterback coach. When Kurt came out of the coach's office, he saw Tom, who had started playing with Kurt's children; we're talking about a getting-down-on-their-level kind of play, a rolling-on-the-ground kind of play. Kurt told me that his first thought was "We need to see more of *that guy*."

The question of how authentic to be in the workplace is a big one. We all know the girl or the guy who comes to work and tells us more than we could ever want to know about her boyfriend, his girlfriend, their hobbies, and their kids. If by chance, you—the reader—and I ever work together, trust me on this: I don't want to hear about how you spent the weekend doing Civil War reenactments. But seeing how the whole team responded when Tom showed us his softer side taught me an important lesson: don't be one guy at work and another guy at home.

12

WHAT I LEARNED FROM MY ELDERS AND BETTERS

Rule #12

Listen to other people, but don't take their opinions for fact.
Have your own experiences. Draw your own conclusions.

URING MY FIRST YEAR in the NFL, the Giants held their training camp at Fairleigh Dickinson University. The campus has multiple fields, and we would alternate between the upper field and the lower field. There were steps that led from one field to the other, but the guys liked to jump a fence between the two. One of the execs, a guy named Rich Donahue, decided to jump the fence but caught his pants and did a face-plant. He wasn't hurt but he was disheveled. It was the funniest thing I'd seen all week, so naturally I laughed, but the rest of the team members and coaches were silent. I looked across the way, and there was only one other guy laughing, one of the reporters who was covering training.

A few hours later, at lunchtime, I was approached by the only other person who'd had the cojones to laugh. That was Jay Glazer, my friend who you may remember constantly needed a ride into the city, the friend who understood the value of play. When we first met, we were both just out of college. He was a little guy who could think fast and talk faster, and he'd talked his way into a job on the Giants in-house newsletter, the *Giants Extra*. A beautiful friendship was formed because a powerful football exec made an ass out of himself and only two guys dared to laugh.

In college, I learned to work with my loneliness, to channel it into fuel on the field. I also got to know and worked with my fear. I was scared to death in college. Now, even as a pro, I may have looked confident on the field, but internally I was terrified. One of the things that defined my friendship with Jay was that he was a guy with whom I never had to pretend not to be lonely, not to be scared. Jay never fit in with the other reporters, in much the same way that, throughout college, I didn't fit in with a lot of the players. We were outsiders, like the characters in S. E. Hinton's classic book, and yet we had somehow made it inside—into the NFL—and we thought that we might be able to take our careers all the way.

I bought a car the year that I got signed: a 1993 Toyota Supra. It was a cool car, but it wasn't extravagant. If I had only three years in the NFL, I didn't want to throw all my money away on the car. Frugal, I drove that car for my first five years in the NFL. But here's something a lot of people don't know; I had a second car, a truck I called "the Tycoon." And whenever someone got within touching distance of the truck, instead of the usual beeping, the car alarm growled, "I know you want to look inside, but please step away from the ride," like a DJ at a club. That truck, which Jay called ghetto, made him laugh so hard. It may have been that the truck was a little bit ghetto. I kept the Supra and got rid of the truck.

. . .

The Supra was all I needed since I didn't get out much due to an injury I sustained in my first year. In my first preseason game, I tore the ligaments in my foot and missed the first five regular-season games. When you're hurt as a professional athlete, you always have to fight the feeling that this could be the end, that the team is moving on without you, that they can't be bothered with you.

Every day, I had to hobble from the field house to the field and back on my crutches. It was a long way. After about two weeks, a car pulled up. The door opened and it was Bob Tisch, who was one of the co-owners of the team. Mr. Tisch looks at me and says, "Get in." And every day, for the next two months, until I was off of those crutches, Mr. Tisch drove me to practice. I was a rookie who had done absolutely nothing for his team. But he gave me a ride, and we developed a friendship that lasted until his death, nearly twenty years later. I loved the conversations that I shared with Mr. Tisch, but I can also look back and see that by treating me so well, even though I was just the new guy—and a new guy with an injury— Mr. Tisch was showing me that by joining the Giants organization, I was joining a family. We spend more time at work than almost anywhere else, and the relationships we build there have an enormous impact on our quality of life. Because I had such a close friendship with my own father, I had a special affinity with the older guys in the league: the owners, the coaches, and the players who had seen so much and were so generous with their time, their wisdom, and their advice.

I'll never forget something that Giants great O.J. Anderson taught me. I was a rookie, sitting around his little cubby with four or five of other guys. It was our first workout together; we hadn't even gone to training camp yet. It turned out to be O.J.'s last year; he didn't even make the team that year, and his career was over. But he passed along something that I use in my life every day. It's not sports related but life related. "You'll hear a lot of things about people," he said. "You'll hear that this guy is so great and this guy's the best and that person is so hard to deal with." O.J. said, "Don't go by any of that. You go on out there and you experience it for yourself and you make your own opinion."

I always return to O.J.'s advice because it applies to so much in life. People try to give you advice to prepare for a situation, but in reality, what they're offering is often hearsay or *their* opinion. It's so easy to psych yourself out and develop limiting thoughts about a person or a situation before you've even encountered it yourself. I've learned to say, "Okay, I hear what you're saying about it, but I need to go and experience it for myself and draw my own conclusions. Because maybe you're overplaying it and maybe you're not. Maybe this was the way it shook out for you, but let me experience it and draw my own conclusions." You can't go by everybody else's opinion all the time. You've just got to go experience things for yourself and form your own.

Harvey Sanders is another older friend who has taught me so much. A businessman who owned the fashion brand Nautica, which helped launch John Varvatos, he's on the board of Under Armour now. Years ago, I would go to the office with him, and what impressed me more than anything as a young guy, not just as an athlete but as someone who hoped to run my own company one day, was that Harvey knew everybody's name. From the biggest sales guy to the guy sweeping the floor, Harvey knew who they were and could greet them by name. It was not only impressive, I saw the effect it had on people. When you take the time to remember names, to learn a little about somebody, and you ask about their hobbies or their spouse or their pets, it says, "I value you." I watched Harvey, and I saw that, sure, most people come to work for the paycheck. But when you take the time to connect to the people around you, you build another level of relationships. There's a feeling of "I would do anything for this person because this person respects and values me." People worked harder for Harvey.

I carry that with me to this day. At *LIVE*, I try to connect with and get to know everyone on our team. I love spending time talking to Estanislao, our janitor. He needs to get a new hat because he walks around the studio with a Jets cap, as if that would ever be okay with me, but besides that, he's my guy. Everyone who answers a phone here at the show, everyone at the front desk, is just as important to this team as the producers and the guests. Nobody's successful by themselves. So for me, it's important that everybody gets treated the same and everybody gets treated with value. If the people around you feel appreciated and are happy that you're there, and they actually want to be a part of whatever team you're building, then they're going to prop you up. They're only going to make this team better. They're going to make you better. They're going to make themselves better. The key is to make each individual feel as if she or he is a valuable asset to the team. In the long run, it benefits everybody.

I met one of my dearest friends at a charity golf outing. Gene Wolfson was building his career in finance. I was building my career in football. At this particular event, each player was assigned to room with a special-invite guest, such as Gene, in a suite. We were put together. On the surface, we could not have been more different. He comes from New Jersey and I come from Texas by way of Germany. He's white and I'm black. That first day, he took the first room and I went back to the second room. There were two single beds, so I did what I always do when the beds are too small for a guy like me; I pushed them together so I could lie on them sideways.

I was exhausted from the flight, so I knocked on Gene's door and told him, "Hey, man, I'm going to take a nap. Can you wake me up at five, so I can get ready for dinner?"

When Gene knocked on the door to wake me up, he saw that I was sleeping on the two single beds. It turns out that the room he was in had a king-size bed and a massive en suite bathroom with a Jacuzzi tub. When we got to dinner, we learned that all the other players had taken the first room and that the special-invite guys had taken the smaller room.

After dinner, Gene was just beside himself. "Man, I'm so sorry," he said. "Let's switch rooms." I told him I appreciated the offer but it wasn't necessary. Had I written him off as a guy with whom I had nothing in common and one who couldn't figure out even the basic decorum for these kinds of events, it would have been my loss. Instead, I waved off the differences in the rooms and started to listen to what he had to say.

Gene and I ended up playing golf together the whole weekend. We stayed in touch and have since become good friends. And while we value our friendship above all else, I can't complain about the sage financial advice I've learned along the way. But more than that, he's taught some fairly memorable life lessons, one of which he learned from Tom Bowes, his first mentor on Wall Street and one of the firm's top-producing brokers.

Back in the day it was customary to eat lunch at your desk, which allowed you to monitor the transactions on the screen and, if necessary, get your shoes shined, all at the same time. Ninety-nine percent of the time, as Gene saw it, a person would get his shoes shined, pay the guy, and barely give the shoeshine man who came directly to your office a second glance. Not Tom.

One afternoon Tom's biggest client called. Gene answered the phone and stalled while he tried to get Tom's attention. Meanwhile, Tom was talking to Ray, the man responsible for his spotless shoes. Once Tom learned who was on the phone, he said, "Tell him I'll call him back in a few minutes." The client kept calling back and, in no time at all, he was agitated because he wanted to put in a big trade. Tom would not pick up the phone. Gene didn't know what to do and, frankly, he was perplexed. He knew that the guy who was calling was a VIP client of Tom's and the one who had the most assets invested with him.

Finally, the client hung up the phone on Gene and Gene was panicking. He kept thinking, "Oh my God, what's going to happen?" When Ray was finally done, Gene rushed into Tom's office. "Tom, why didn't you pick up the phone? That was your biggest client." Tom said, "I was talking to Ray about his finances. Every day he comes in and he gives me half of what he made and I put it away for him." Gene still didn't get it. "But, Tom, that was your *biggest* client." Tom used to call Gene "Wolf," short for his last name, Wolfson. Tom just looked at Gene and said, "Wolf, Ray's assets are no less important to him than is the money of the client who was just on the line." Gene remembers just sitting back in his chair and thinking, "Holy crap. That's a life lesson for me."

Gene never forgot that story, and once he shared it with me, I never forgot the lesson either. It doesn't matter whether you have two million dollars with your financial adviser or two hundred dollars, it's important to *you*. It's a lesson about what you should look for in a financial adviser, but it's also a life lesson in how you should treat people. Like Maya Angelou famously said, "I've learned that people will forget what you said, people will forget what you did, but people will never forget how you made them feel."

Artie Rabin is a little younger than my dad, but he runs around like he's younger than me. Artie is the Pied Piper of people. Artie's biggest thrill is to make sure everybody is happy. He is a sharer of his success. He's not somebody who has been successful and plays it close to his vest, as in "You know what, this is mine and I won't let you have a peek." If he can share a contact or a lesson he's learned and save you the trouble of making an unnecessary misstep, he will. If you mention being overworked or exhausted, Artie will say, "Go out to my weekend place. The house is yours." Sometimes you go out there and there are twenty people staying out there, because for Artie, there is no such thing as a closed door. Whenever he has a party, you always meet the most interesting range of people: everyone from people in their seventies and eighties down to young couples with newborn babies. He's not about status or class. He's a collector of fun people, and I've tried to do the same.

Not too long ago, I rented a house in Mexico and hosted an assortment of friends. We didn't even leave the house: just swam in the pool, ate good food, and talked all night. The setting was luxurious, but the fun was basic and inclusive. Artie taught me that.

Sometimes people will meet my friends, and they ask, "What do you do?" This is often code for "Do you have any money?" I don't care what my friends do for a living or if they make a lot of money. It's about the quality of the person. My friend Gary is a struggling comedian. When we go out to dinner, I treat. He did this joke in his routine recently about how I invited him to hang out with me for the weekend. He took a not very glamorous Greyhound bus from Los Angeles to meet us in Vegas, then he stayed in a fancy suite on the floor we'd rented, and then he flew back to L.A. on a private plane. Gary says, "My bank account needs to catch up with my lifestyle." Which is hilarious—and true.

I also have no doubt that Gary's bank account will eventually catch up with his lifestyle; he's talented. I go to his shows. Sometimes when I show up at a little comedy club, the owners are shocked. They say, "Why are *you* here?" I'm Gary's friend. Why wouldn't I go and support what he does? He watches everything I do. He supports me. My work is on a bigger platform now, but it's not any different. It's all relative. What I love about having older friends like Harvey and Artie, and Deacon before them, is that they show me that the best is truly yet to come. I'm looking forward to building and growing and traveling and celebrating with my friends for decades to come.

13

CHANGE BEFORE
YOU HAVE TO

Rule #13

Too late is in the grave . . . The decade ahead might hold more
possibility than we previously imagined.

JACK WELCH, the legendary businessman and former chair of
GE, said that among his best business advice to anyone was
"Change before you have to." As an athlete, I became a master
at making small changes: changing my diet, changing my workout,
changing the way I approached a certain play or offensive move. But
I'm also a guy who played fifteen years for the same team. That's
almost unheard of in professional sports. So in a lot of ways, I'm like
the guy who spent his entire career at the post office. I knew the ter-
rain, liked the regular paycheck, didn't want to make any changes.
On the other hand, like a corporate employee who can see that his

company is restructuring. I knew that there was a ticking clock on my career and that, like it or not, in give or take five years, I would be out of a job. My career was winding down. So after more than a dozen years in the league, I began thinking about what I consider the two essential questions to making a big job change: when do I want to leave this job and what am I going to do next?

This chapter is really about the first question: Do I want to leave this job? Because that one question is really a suitcase that is packed with a dozen more questions. Once you've decided that you're going to change jobs, a lot of questions come up: How much longer *can* I do this job? How can I use the time I have now to prepare myself for this transition? How can I get everything I can out of my current job so that I'm ready for the next one? Sometimes you're just ready to jump ship, to leap and see what's in store for you. But I think of my life in chapters, and while not every chapter has a happy ending, it's my goal to end each chapter of my life—be it a home renovation or the end of a particular relationship or work partnership—with a sense of grace and accomplishment.

I had something particularly ambitious in mind for the last page of the last chapter of my career as an athlete: I wanted to win the Super Bowl. Every year hundreds of great athletes, guys who set records, develop signature moves, and earn their place in the sports history books, retire without that elusive Super Bowl ring. For a while, it seemed like I was destined to be one of those guys. Yet just when I sensed I had more time playing professionally behind me than ahead of me, I decided to grab the wheel and do everything I could to steer myself toward the goal of a Super Bowl win. My situation may seem unique, but when I talk to friends, they often talk about a similar desire to go out on top: maybe it's wanting to leave a job after being the top salesperson in the division and getting the Hawaiian vacation that goes with that distinction, so they can take their family on an amazing trip before venturing into something new. They dig deep one more time. Or the small-business owner who puts his or her kids through college and then decides to retire and take life as it comes.

When I played football, my evolution from being the rookie, to being a reliable and consistent player, to becoming one of the team's leaders was slow: the guys had to experience for themselves how I played, my work ethic, how I showed up on and off the field, before they put their faith in me. I didn't mind. I observed that in the military. You can't ask somebody to lift you up, to leapfrog you to the front of the line; what you do will always matter more than what you say. It's like the James Baldwin quote, "Children have never been very good at listening to their elders, but they have never failed to imitate them."

Now, as team leader, I had to figure out how to motivate our players. One morning as we set out to practice, I started literally jumping up and down in the huddle, urging the players to join me in a simulation of stomping out the opponent. I'm a big guy, but I would bounce in the air as if I were jumping on a trampoline. "Do you know what we do?" I'd scream. "We stomp you out." It became my motto and one of the rituals I put into place to bring order to the day. Earlier I wrote about the power of routine. My pregame routine was extensive.

First, before each game, I would swing by the equipment room and get my ankles taped. There was a ritual, a method, a pace, and an order to how I put on my pads, my pants, my socks, how I wrapped my fingers up, how I put my wrist braces on. It's called protective gear, and as I put each item on, I visualized the equipment doing its job, keeping me healthy and safe.

Then I'd sit down and read the program for that day's game. I actually read the program and looked at all the players on my team and looked at all the players on the other team. Just looked at their pictures, visualized us on the field, took in who I was playing with and who I was playing against.

After I examined the program, taking the time to look at the pictures of all the players, even my own team, whose pictures I know, whose pictures wouldn't change the whole year, it was time for one more DJ moment. Harder hip-hop now. 50 Cent. Snoop Dogg. Death Row. 2Pac. I'd put that music on, and I'd walk through the locker room making sure that I took a moment to connect with every player, every coach, either by shaking every single person's hand or giving him a pat on the back. No one was excluded, neither the equipment staff nor the trainers nor the doctors.

I wanted them to know that I held myself accountable to each and every one of them. We were all in this machine, this Big Blue Wrecking Crew, and I touched every piece of this machine because I couldn't be the piece that broke. I would be accountable and reliable to them with my performance. This showed that it's about team and not any individual. We needed to work together.

Jessie Armstead let me know, "When you came out of Texas Southern, there were doubts about you, just like there are for any player who comes out of a small school. Then you got hurt, and they wondered if you could hold up physically. But not only did you hold up, but you kept getting better and better."

Right before each game, Jessie and I would stand in the tunnel and say, "You and me." A lot of the guys go through the tunnel feeling that they are alone. But I knew I could count on Jessie. I was so appreciative of that.

After we defeated the Green Bay Packers to claim the NFC championship, the opponent we needed to stomp out in order to claim Super Bowl victory was the undefeated Patriots. The mighty Tom Brady was out to join Terry Bradshaw and Joe Montana in an exalted pantheon of three: the only quarterbacks to have won four Super Bowls.

The biggest thing for me, in sports and in life, is respect. In football, every Monday you go into a meeting and watch a tape of the last game you and your team played. Your teammates are watching you play on that tape, as is the opposing team that you just played. So, for that matter, is the team you're going to play in three weeks, four weeks. That tape is an extension of you; it's your stand-in.

I never wanted anyone to look at my performance on one of those tapes and say, "He quits." Never. Even if we were losing, I still went hard. There were games in which we didn't have a chance, and the coach would want to pull me out to prevent injury and preserve one of his star players for future games. I'd say, "No, I was in the game when we got behind. I'll be in the game until the end." I needed my teammates to look at me on the field and respect that I was there. I wanted other players to watch me on tape and say, "I heard about him, but he was better than I expected. I have more respect for him now because I see how thorough he is." That was my thing then and it's my thing now. You are not going to leave any interaction with me and say I didn't leave it all on the table. You're going to pop in that tape of my playing and you're going to see a guy that goes 100 percent, from start to finish.

In sports, you develop a level of amnesia that protects you and helps you to achieve. You can't think about what happened on the field five minutes ago, because it's in the past and you can't change it. So that bad play we just had? What can we do? We can't do anything. The *next* play? Anything can happen.

Time and again, we'd have a bad play. I'd rally the guys to look forward, not back; then we'd go out there, and the other team would fumble the ball. It's a great lesson. Each step, each day, each moment is an opportunity for something good to happen, even though something bad happened just before it. But the key is this: anything can happen, good can and does follow bad, *as long as you don't give up.*

Following the playoff game with the Packers, we went from a feeling of "We hope we win" the Super Bowl to "We expect to win," even though the odds were stacked against us. It's not a big shift, just a little adjustment of the mind yet it's crucial. Before we went onto the field, I also encouraged everyone to wear the mantle of urgency with a certain lightness. I had tried to push myself toward victory several years earlier with a kind of miserable, blind-to-everything-but-winning willpower—and guess what? It didn't work. This time, I kept telling the guys, "Don't worry. We got this. Have fun. This is the Super Bowl."

I also urged the players to claim it. My dad always taught me to say, "When, not if." I remember telling the guys, "You've already won the game. The score is going to be 17–14. Believe it and it will happen." Then we won: the Super Bowl that everyone thought we'd lose. And the score was 17–14.

. . .

After the Super Bowl win, I took a few months to reflect and decided to retire. A few months after that, the Giants offered me a sweetened contract to come back for one more year. In my heart, I wanted to stay retired. I remember Howie Long saying to me, "Okay. Let me tell you something. When it ends, you don't know when it will go." He said, "You don't know when your game is going to go. You don't know if it's going to be at training camp. You don't know if it's going to be at the beginning of the season, the middle of the season, or the end of the season. But when your game goes, it goes fast."

That always scared the hell out of me. Like you're out there, and all of a sudden you realize that the guys you used to throw around, you can't throw them around anymore. The guys who used to not be able to block you in certain ways are suddenly, effectively keeping you down. The speed you formerly used to have to be able to catch somebody, you don't have it anymore.

I started experiencing exactly what Howie had put into words. I said, "Man. He's right." I could feel it. Plenty of new guys had come into the league before, but I was always able to hold my own. Now I started to see guys enter the league who were faster than me. Guys whose athleticism was a challenge. I started thinking, "This guy is a rookie or a second- or third-year player?!" Having to keep up with the rookies helped me up my game. But it also made me realize that I'm mortal. It made me realize that I was slowing down. I could see little slips. Not noticeable to others, perhaps, but I just knew that I had to work that much harder to stay or to get a little bit better. More, the harder work was making me only incrementally better. That's when I started to realize it was time to consider moving on. One of the most dangerous things about being an athlete isn't playing. It's not knowing when to stop.

Over the course of fifteen years, I blew my lower back out countless times, and while I didn't go to medical school, I can tell you that I've suffered permanent damage to my sacroiliac joint as well as my fourth and fifth lumbar vertebrae. I still remember the first time that someone had to put my socks on for me. The operative word being "first." Imagine being thirty years old and needing somebody to put your socks on for you. I've dislocated every single one of my fingers. A sprained knee cost me a game not once but twice, and I injured both the AC joints in my shoulder. I tore my pectoral muscle in my chest, and once I was whacked in the shin so hard that I have an indentation in my bone that the doctors say will never heal. The irony is that I was one of the lucky ones. No concussions, no life-threatening spinal cord injury, no paralysis. Talk about counting your blessings. Thank God.

The game had given me everything I'd ever hoped to achieve: the chance to make records; the opportunity to play with legends; and the chance to play in the Super Bowl and win that elusive ring. But there's also a toll the NFL takes on your body. Your back, hips, knees, shoulders, and neck don't work like they used to, leaving you to figure out a way around it, to compensate physically. My game was going, yes, but wasn't the Super Bowl proof that my game wasn't yet completely gone? I debated: do I play another year? It was when I was deliberating with my dad that it came to me. There's a scene at the end of the film *Babe* where the farmer tells Babe, "That'll do, pig. That'll do." My dad said the equivalent: "There's no need to do that anymore." When he said that, I immediately felt I didn't have to prove anymore that I could do what he sent me to do all those years ago. That's when I realized I was done.

I told the Giants that I was not going to return to football and thanked them, sincerely, for all the organization had ever done for me. "You've been a great Giant. I think you've done more for us than we can ever do for you," owner John Mara said. In the end, I went to seven Pro Bowls and recorded the fifth most sacks in NFL history during my career. I was thirty-six years old.

I knew I would miss the game, yet I promised myself that I wouldn't shed a tear. So many guys begin their retirement speech stoically and seriously and then end it crying like a baby. If you're crying like that, maybe it's not time to retire. Personally, I felt as if a weight had been lifted from my shoulders. If you could have seen what was going on in my head at that podium, you would have seen banners and floats and balloons and clowns. I felt like there was value to leaving when I still had the ability to play, to be one of the best.

Walking away from the game meant walking away from millions of dollars on the table. But it had never been about the money. Usually in sports you go out when they tell you to go out. I had this golden-ticket opportunity to leave when I wanted to leave. It took courage to retire when there was still gas in the tank, when I knew I could still play at a very high level. But I wanted to be smart. I came into the league as a naïve kid; I wanted to leave as an elite athlete who had learned a thing or two.

Not that it was easy emotionally. As a football player, you feel like a gladiator. You feel unstoppable. Kids look up to you. Adults look up to you. You play in stadiums where crowds of seventy to eighty thousand people cheer you on and millions more watch you on television. Heck, the City of New York even threw a ticker tape parade for the Giants! There were "Michael Strahan for President" signs, and bales of confetti were streaming through the air! That's tough to walk away from. Even just a regular game—any given

Sunday, so to speak—can be addictive. You stand in the tunnel and you're all suited up for battle. It's quiet in there. You can hear the sound of your breath, and if you whisper, it echoes. Then you run out onto the field, and the sensation and noise of thousands of fans, screaming, talking, waiting for you, just hits you. There are fireworks and marching bands every single time you walk out onto the field. But as my friend Howie Long explained, "The minute you retire, all of it stops. Immediately. Instantaneously." When I retired at thirty-six, I had to ask myself the question that we all do when one big chapter of our lives closes and we don't know what the next chapter will hold. What now?

For a while, I couldn't entirely fathom what came next. Transitions are hard and inevitably include a moment of regret. I knew that all those guys were at the Giants training camp. I was still in good shape. It would have been the easiest thing to pick up the phone and call Tom Coughlin and John Mara and say, "You know what, guys, let's do it again." Though I knew it wasn't in my best interest to play anymore—I had my health, that Super Bowl ring, money in the bank, which would allow me to take care of my family—still, every morning at six A.M., I had to shake the feeling, had to stop looking at my watch wondering if I was going to be five minutes early or whether I was going to be fined. I had to stop the kind of running daydream that I started to have in which I was all suited up and there I was, running out of the tunnel with my uniform on. I had to get okay with the fact that it just wasn't going to happen again.

So many Americans know what it's like to have to reinvent themselves when everything they've known and taken comfort in is no longer available to them, to try to find what positive psychologist Mihaly Csikszentmihalyi calls "flow" more than once, maybe even multiple times. I've seen it with friends and family who struggled through Hurricanes Katrina and Sandy. I've seen it in young vets who maybe joined the military at the age of eighteen or nineteen and retire twenty years later—not yet forty years old but having to start over from scratch. I was lucky to retire from football at the age of thirty-six, to have it be my choice, with no major injuries and without management pushing me out. But I still had to figure out what to do. Like every person who has had to reinvent themselves careerwise, I didn't want to just sit home and do nothing. I love golf, but even *I* couldn't play golf all day, every day. I had to find my purpose, which meant that I needed to go out of my comfort zone.

My body had dictated when it was time for me to make a transition. Others shift, sometimes unconsciously, decade by decade. It's what the British historian Ferdinand Mount is credited with calling "decaditis": the urge to separate the experience of our lives into ten-year chunks. That was the path of my business partner Constance Schwartz. A badass in the best sense of the word, she had a notable career in the NFL. Ten years later, Snoop approached her to be his manager. Rather than stay in the NFL, where she was content and collecting a regular paycheck, she took a risk on herself, immersing herself in worlds in which she had no experience: hip-hop, Long Beach, the music industry. She led the charge to make Snoop a global icon and household name while keeping his voice authentic. Needless to say, she was having a blast. Ten years in, I was fortunate that she was ready to change. We decided to go into partnership together and have not looked back. I think it's especially interesting that Constance shifted gears in her career decade by decade: In her twenties, she worked in the NFL. In her thirties, she worked in the music industry. When she turned forty, she decided to come work with me. For many of us, a big birthday can be an opportunity to do a much-needed check-in. How's it going? What have I learned and accomplished in this decade? What do I want to learn and accomplish in the next?

Sometimes the transition isn't our choice: so many people know what it's like to be laid off or downsized. But the best times, I think, are when you feel the need to make a change and you take the steps to make it happen. Like Jack Welch said, "Change before you have to." The good news—scratch that, the great news is that it's never too late. Life expectancy in the United States is at an all-time high. Many of us can expect to have vital, healthy, creative work lives into our sixties and our seventies. (I'm personally hoping to retire *waaay* before then, but I'm a guy who currently has three jobs, so believe me when I say I like the idea of options.)

I know some of you are thinking, "Sure, change is easy if you're a twentysomething who can go back home and live with Mom and Dad. It's much harder if you're in your thirties or forties or even older, right?" But as Barack Obama so famously said, "While we breathe, we hope." I deeply believe that as long as we are breathing, there is hope for us to do more, be more, have and enjoy more.

Hope paired with planning, of course, is even more effective.

What's exciting is that the research shows that there are so many Americans who are planning in advance, no matter their age, to live a happier life. *USA Today* recently published a survey that found that one in three pre-retirees—people in their fifties—are planning to change careers in the next five years. They want to take the experience and the know-how they've built up in their current jobs and apply it to a new career. The survey found that for many of these people— who fully expect to work another twenty or twenty-five years—the quest is to find something meaningful that gives them both increased satisfaction but also a sense of purpose. The survey found that among fiftysomethings: "82% want to give back more, 80% want to shift gears and pursue a passion, and 74% want to travel more."

I know that every day people can change careers and find even greater happiness in their work life because I saw it in my own father. After he retired from the military, when he was in his fifties, he and my mother, a stay-at-home mom, decided to remain in Germany, where they opened a trucking business, with which they transported furniture and cars across Europe. In the early nineties, when Yugoslavia was going through the terrible conflict and ethnic cleansing under Milošević, my parents used their trucks to deliver humanitarian goods and donations from Germany to war-torn regions in Eastern Europe.

One of my favorite stories on the subject of "it's never too late" comes from Po Bronson's groundbreaking book, *What Should I Do with My Life?* In it, he tells the story of a British chemistry professor who decided to become a lawyer in his sixties. Sidney Ross, as Bronson explains, spent twenty-seven years as a university professor. He had tenure; he thought his job was his for life. Then he was pushed into early retirement. The payout for over a quarter of a century's worth of work: roughly forty thousand dollars. It wouldn't take Sidney and his wife into their old age, but it was enough for Sidney to revisit an old dream. He had always loved the law. So he went to law school, where he excelled. The trouble began after his second year, when he needed to find an internship at a law firm. It was like that Vince Vaughn–Owen Wilson movie *The Internship*. Nobody wants to give an older guy the chance to be an intern. In this case, Sidney Ross was old enough to be his fellow interns' grandfather. Finally, he found one firm willing to let him do some clerical work in the basement for the summer. Sidney was disappointed, but he decided to give it a shot.

All summer he worked hard, but not being able to really work on cases was difficult for him. "I had moments of depression as others got 'the shot' on interesting work. I didn't think I was entitled. I believed I would succeed on my merits eventually." One afternoon, he noticed that his boss had been contracted to write a textbook, and from the notes on the desk, he saw that the guy hadn't even begun writing. Sidney offered to help, explaining that he'd published over sixty articles and two chemistry books. The editorial work led to work on actual fraud cases, and by the time the internship was over, Sidney's cases had taken him as far as Singapore and Hong Kong. Even more, he was offered a permanent position at the firm. Sidney Ross told Po Bronson that he went from being "pariah to jewel in the crown." In his seventies now and still a little incredulous that he could make such a tremendous change in careers, Ross says he loves the life of a big city lawyer.

"Too late is in the grave," my parents always told me, and stories like Sidney Ross's prove how true that is. I know that for so many of us, changing gears in our career isn't easy. But I think we all owe it to ourselves to take the quiet time to ask ourselves, "If I could do anything, what kind of work would I be doing?" Maybe, like it did for Sidney Ross, the decade ahead might hold more possibility than we previously imagined. I also believe that not everyone needs to do a 180-degree change to find more happiness. Look around your own company. Pema Chödrön, the Buddhist scholar, says, "Nothing goes away until it has taught us what we need to know." What about your current position can teach you what you need to know?

Do some research on what new opportunities might be opening up in your line of work. Maybe greater happiness and more prosperity for you is a matter of pivoting, not quitting. Never before in our human history have there been so many different ways to make a living. When the first U.S. Census was taken, there were 322 job titles listed. On the most recent U.S. Census, there were 31,000 types of jobs to choose from.

Newly retired, I had to figure out which one of those thirty-plus thousand was the right one for me.

14

CURIOSITY AND VISUALIZATION

Rule #14

If you can dream it, you can achieve it. Use
visualization to access it.

READ RECENTLY THAT the average child will ask forty thousand
questions between the ages of two and five. But an interesting
thing starts to happen once a kid enters preschool: the number of
questions she or he asks starts to decrease. It makes no sense—the
school is full of interesting, cool, fun things with which to play and
stimulate kids' brains, and they are surrounded by other smart children, yet they ask fewer and fewer questions. What scientists found
is that it's not that kids are less curious, it's that they grow more
uncomfortable with their curiosity in a school environment. Matt
Groening, the creator of *The Simpsons,* points out that "It seems the

main rule that traditional schools teach is how to sit in rows quietly, which is perfect training for grown-up work in a dull office or factory, but not so good for education."

Of course, that's not the case at home, as I can attest with Sophia and Isabella. Anyone who has ever seen Louis C.K.'s "Why" routine knows that kids and their endless questions can drive you *nuts* as a parent. But curiosity, the desire and ability to ask questions, is a muscle that we can't afford to let atrophy if we want to live our best lives. Brian Grazer, the award-winning movie producer, defines curiosity as an essential trait to his success. He says that it's the conversations he has with people and the questions he asks that have shaped his career: "Being interested in other fields and meeting experts outside entertainment—whether it's a two-hour conversation with John Nash that turns into *A Beautiful Mind,* or talking to people in architecture or fashion, CIA directors or Nobel laureates—has given me a better sense of which ideas feel authentic and new. Also, if you're engaging in these conversations, you're becoming a better, smarter, more interesting person, which gives you an endless amount of confidence. When everyone in the business is trying to work with Tom Hanks or Russell Crowe or Denzel Washington or Eddie Murphy, I think I get the tip on the ball because they know I care about more than just the dynamics of Hollywood."

In his book *A More Beautiful Question,* journalist and innovation expert Warren Berger reminds us, "In our lives, in general, there's a tendency to move along on autopilot when we really ought to be in the habit of regularly stepping back and questioning everything—about our career choices, about our attitudes and beliefs, about the ways we choose to live. Questioning is good for us. It can help to open up new possibilities in our lives. It's a first step in solving problems. It makes us more successful as leaders. People who ask a lot of questions tend to be more engaged in their lives, more fulfilled, and happier."

When I look back, I can see that even when I was in the midst of some of my biggest successes, I was still asking questions, still looking for opportunities to grow. My seventh year in the NFL was a great one. I went to the Pro Bowl that year, and we played the San Francisco 49ers on Monday night. I got two sacks that game. I was up to ten sacks for the season, which was great.

I was kicking butt that season, but still I didn't feel that I'd reached my maximum, and I wasn't sure how to tap into whatever else I had to give. The team flew to Tucson, to the University of Arizona, to stay for the week and practice instead of traveling back to New York, since our next game was in Arizona, against the Cardinals. While I was on campus, I went to see a therapist, a guy who specialized in meditation and creative visualization.

We were sitting in his small office, and even though I didn't know this guy from Adam, I totally opened up. I told him, "When I close my eyes, I can see myself lining up on the field. I see myself beat the guy in front of me, but right before I hit the quarterback, I can't finish the play in my head. It goes dark. The visualization ends." I explained that it was bugging me because I was having a great year but I didn't feel like I had all the confidence I could summon. I had more in the tank but I couldn't access it.

He made a tape for me and he said, "Michael, I want you to listen to this tape at least two or three nights a week, before you go to bed. If you fall asleep, it's no big deal because your subconscious never sleeps."

Intrigued, I started listening to the tape that night, and right away the positive messages reaffirmed my confidence. I learned how to relax. It all starts with breathing, taking a deep breath in, deep breath out. Sure, I'd heard it before, but the tape reminded me; it all starts by connecting with your breath.

That Sunday, we played the Arizona Cardinals. I went out and had the best, most perfectly executed game I can ever remember. I could vividly visualize every play exactly in my mind. I felt like I knew what the other players would do before they even did it. I played, mentally, on a whole different level. Physically, I felt amazing. But mentally, I was in the super zone. It was the best I've ever been on the football field.

I played over two hundred pro games in my career. I can remember moments from almost every one. But Arizona, I can remember the *whole* game, from the starting kickoff to the final touchdown.

One of my friends, Harvey Sanders, former CEO and president of Nautica Corporation, who watched all of my games like a coach, always says, even now, "Michael, that game in Arizona was the best game you've ever played." He doesn't know anything about the tape. (Though I guess now the whole world will know about my tape.) But whenever he mentions Arizona, I always tell him, "Yeah, Harvey, it was, the best I've ever *felt.*"

I listened to that tape, night after night, for years. Any time I was in a corner—I was injured, going through drama with my coach or in my marriage, afraid that I was going to be one of those guys who played a great career but retired without a Super Bowl ring—I'd listen to the tape and be reaffirmed about the depth of potential that is present in all of us.

My teammates Michael Barrow and Cedric Jones and I used to all the time ride to the hotel together on Saturdays, then to the game on Sunday morning. Always interested in improving himself, Michael Barrow approached me one day and said, "Tell me about this motivational tape." I handed him my Walkman (yes, this was back in the days of cassette tapes).

I said, "Here, I'll let you listen so you get the idea of it."

He loved it.

Then I said, "Well, you know, if you want, I'll give you the guy's number."

The next day, when I gave him the number, he said, "No. I'm good. I made my own."

I was perplexed.

Michael Barrow had recorded himself whispering all of these inspirational phrases. It was comical—and kind of creepy. But that was Michael. Determined to better himself but cheap as hell.

There are so many options out there today for motivational mantras that you can listen to for serenity and inspiration—from Tony Robbins to Oprah and Deepak. But do me a favor. Don't just bootleg your own. Support the positive economy, people! Buy the tape!

Because I listened to it for years, I don't even need the tape anymore. When I need to visualize a goal, I just sit quietly, connect to my breath, and relax myself. The therapist also taught me a visualization exercise: you connect your index finger to your thumb and imagine that it's a steel ring. Hold the posture as tight as you can and picture this as solid steel, impenetrable and unbreakable, a symbol of your goals or resolve. Now if I'm nervous, I do the gesture and I picture a steel ring and it reminds me, "You got this. You're solid."

Although I didn't know it at the time, visualization has been credited with helping everyone from athletes and musicians to surgeons and technicians. Malcolm Gladwell, the *New Yorker* writer, studied the power of visualization and found, "When psychologists study people who are expert at motor tasks, they find that almost all of them use their imaginations in a very particular and sophisticated way . . . Jack Nicklaus, for instance, has said that he has never taken a swing that he didn't first rehearse frame by frame in his mind. Yo-Yo Ma told me that he remembers riding on a bus, at the age of seven, and solving a difficult musical problem by visualizing himself playing the piece on the cello. Dr. Charlie Wilson (a neurosurgeon) talks about how he would go running in the morning and review each day's operation in his head. 'It was a virtual rehearsal,' he says, 'so when I was actually doing the operation, it was as if I were doing it for the second time.' "

So how can you use visualization in your own life?

- **Mentally rehearse the big moment.** Be it a job interview or a presentation or any other kind of high-pressure task, picture yourself completing the task. Take your time, find a quiet space, and imagine how you will look, what you want to say, how you want to feel. Scientists say that the more you picture yourself doing a task, the more your brain begins to believe that the task is easy and manageable. It's like Dr. Charlie Wilson imagining the surgery before it happens. By the time the moment comes, you walk into the room with more confidence and the feeling that you've been there before, because mentally you have.

- **Do more than see it.** For visualization to be even more effective, don't just use your sense of sight, use all five senses. The more you can close your eyes and make the moment real, the more powerful the visualization becomes. When our ancestors lived closer to the land, they used all of their senses because their survival depended on it: they needed every one of the amazing tools our brain comes preloaded with to find food, survive danger, and build community. Because we live in a very different world, we tend to underutilize our senses, but the more real you can make it in your mind, the more real you can make it in real life.

- **Program your dreams.** One of the reasons that my tape was so effective is that I listened to it at night, before I fell asleep. During the day, we tend to be busy and distracted. At night, right before we fall asleep, our thoughts tend to slow down and we're more open to the unconscious benefits of visualization.

  My brother Victor is two years older than me. Ever since I was a little boy, we were always close. We have a lot in common, and one of those things is a love of cars. As kids, we used to buy every car magazine we could get our hands on. We read them over and over again, until they were practically falling apart. Then one day my mother said to me, "All these years, the two of you have been spending your money on magazines, hundreds of dollars a year. If you'd saved that money and put it together, you could actually have bought yourselves a car." It was such a huge revelation to me. I thought, "You know what? She's right." My mentality changed to "I love looking at cars. I love imagining myself in these cars. But now I've got to close the magazine and figure out a way to get one." Which is to say visualization won't get you all the way.

  For so many of us, there's a disconnect between hoping and

actually taking the steps necessary to make whatever it is we hope for a reality. Using the methodologies, the rituals, the positive thinking I've outlined in this book, I try to stomp out the disconnect between hope and activation and build specific plans to close the gap (no pun intended).

15

RENOVATING ONE'S LIFE

Rule #15

Don't approach your personal renovation without the right partner in your corner, not only encouraging you but also telling you the hard stuff, someone who will be brutally honest with you.

AFTER IMPLEMENTING THE strategies I've laid out, such as having a few lines in the water, as I reference in chapter 2, using visualization techniques to envision what it was that I wanted to do with my future, I decided to pursue a career in television. There's a side of me that is a real introvert. I take in energy when I'm alone. But there's another part of me that is enlivened and energized when I am interacting with others. I first tapped into that side of myself when Jay Glazer invited me to this speaking gig at a synagogue in Long Island. I was cool with that. I've got the military kid thing nailed down; I can get along with anyone. The youngest person in the audience that day was about eighty-two. I was cool with that too. I don't remember exactly what I said to them. I remember keeping it real, talking to them as if they were my parents and their friends and we were all sitting around the table playing cards in Houston. I was bringing the house down when suddenly Jay got nervous. He passed me a note that said, "Stop making them laugh so hard. These old people are a cough away from a heart attack." The feeling I got when I connected with them was something that I wanted to explore more. Broadcast, the field in which I was gaining some experience, especially at FOX, seemed like a good fit.

Although it appears as if I jumped seamlessly from the NFL to FOX Sports to *LIVE* with Kelly, in reality that couldn't be further from the truth. I remember doing shows that nobody would see—either because my bit was edited out or because the show was canceled before it was broadcast. The first time I was ever asked to interview anybody was when the local FOX station called me and asked me if I wanted to go to the *Sports Illustrated* party for their swimsuit issue. Who wouldn't? I walked around, just happy to be there, thrilled for the perk. Then when I least expected it someone put a microphone in my hand and told me to interview the models. It turns out they didn't just want me to have a good time, they were putting me to work. Words tumbled and stumbled out of my mouth; if I'm honest, I didn't make much sense—in fact, I was hopeless. God knows, I hope nobody ever finds that footage, because I was so nervous and so bad that the supermodel Vendela Kirsebom took hold of the situation by grabbing the microphone and interviewing me. Bless her!

Things got better when I did a series called the *Best Damn Sports Show Period* with Tom Arnold, John Salley, Rodney Peete, Chris

Rose, Charissa Thompson, and Rob Dibble. On the show, ex–hockey, football, and basketball players talked, joked, and mixed it up with the main host. I had fun, and it was an immersion course on getting comfortable in front of a camera. I would do a quick ten- or fifteen-minute hit from New York when I wasn't able to travel to Los Angeles, which taught me to sit and interact with a camera without being able to see the reaction of the other host, and how to create energy with facial expressions as well as words. I also learned on that show how to laugh at myself. We were doing Halloween shows, and one time, they sent me a costume—it was a giant tooth. I'm sitting there doing this show in this giant tooth with my head popping out. I was Count Gap-ula. The April Fools' Day prank in which Tom Arnold and I pretended to get into a knock-down, drag-out bar brawl still ranks as one of my favorite memories. (You can look it up on YouTube.) At the time, I was still playing football. I hadn't a clue that a job could be so much fun.

As Jay grew in his broadcasting career, he always brought me in as one of his first guests on whatever show he was hosting. So it was a lot of fun when we took over as cohosts of the Spike TV show *Pros vs. Joes*. On the show, three professional athletes, the "Pros" took on three average guys, the "Joes," in a series of challenges. If the Joes bested the pros, they won ten thousand dollars.

Just when it appeared I was making headway, however, I encountered another setback. I appeared on a sitcom called *Brothers*. It ran only one season, but it might as well have been a graduate program in broadcast television. I learned about memorizing scripts, comedic timing, multiple takes, and interacting with true actors. The show was developed by Don Reo, who created the Chris Rock show *Everybody Hates Chris,* and it starred me as a former NFL star player (not a big stretch there) and Daryl "Chill" Mitchell as my brother, whose once promising football career ended after a tragic accident left him paralyzed. The great CCH Pounder played our mother and Carl "Apollo Creed" Weathers played our dad. It was canceled after just one season, and though it was a career setback (there went my embryonic acting career), to my mind, it was in no way a failure. It was a line in the water.

In the first few years after I retired from the Giants, Constance and I were bootstrapping. Even though I was working at FOX I wanted to be more involved in business and television. I needed to find my new set point. I could see myself working in broadcast, but how could I stomp out the gap between seeing it and doing it? Our production company was in an office borrowed from a friend. There were just the two of us and an intern who answered the phones. We kept our expenses to a minimum—we didn't want to go over budget on this renovation we called my career. So we had some of our best meetings not at fancy restaurants, but at the International House of Pancakes— i.e., IHOP. One idea we mapped out at the IHOP—where my savvy friend and business partner would bring her own 100 percent pure Vermont maple syrup—was a talk show in which I would cohost with one or two other people. We put feelers out and waited for the phone to ring. Walk in the park, right? By now, after all, I had had some television experience and had vastly improved from the time I couldn't even interview a model at the *SI* swimsuit party.

Not at all. Not only did the phone not ring. The response was so lackluster one Hollywood personality went so far as to tell us she'd be doing us a favor to even take the meeting and hung up before we could utter a polite thank-you.

As I say in chapter 10, good can and *will* follow bad. After being dissed by the A list, the B list, and the C list in Hollywood, I got a call to fill in as a guest cohost for *LIVE* with the incredibly skilled Kelly Ripa. And I learned something from the experience. I realized, with hindsight, that in figuring out what my post-football life was going to look like, I was renovating my career from the ground up. And I know a thing or two about renovation.

I've renovated almost every home that I've lived in over the past fifteen years. Some hate the process; I love it, perhaps because it reminds me of team sports, where everyone needs to work together to create the flow that makes the project come together seamlessly. You can't put in a basement media room unless you make sure the basement is free of mildew and moisture. The painter can't start painting until the electrician has wired the house and closed up the walls. I've come to see the choreography of it all as akin not just to football and other team sports but also to life, particularly when it comes to architecting your second or third act. It's a life lesson about dreams and executing those dreams. Anyone who's ever renovated a house will give you some tips about what they learned in the process. Here are my top five tips for renovating, indeed transforming your life.

1. INFRASTRUCTURE IS EVERYTHING

When you're renovating a house, you learn that while you want to focus on the exterior and superficial aspects—the beautiful lighting, the breathtaking pool—you've got to start with the basics, the foundation, the plumbing, the electricals. If you don't get your priorities straight, you will ultimately spend more money circling back to replace old pipes or fix faulty wiring that you should have replaced from the start.

For me, taking the time to fix the stuff you can't see meant taking the time to really work on my relationships with my family and friends; being on the road, chasing glory on the gridiron, meant that I wasn't always around to spend real quality time with the people I loved.

Before I started to test out what my next career move might be, I took the time to work on my personal life, to make sure that my infrastructure was tight, because first and foremost, my number one goal in life is to be a loving dad, a father to Tanita, Michael Junior, Isabella, and Sophia. If nothing else happened for me, I figured I could sit on the beach in California and enjoy life with my four kids. As long as I had enough money to get them through school, as long as I could muster the will and the skill to help them set sail toward their biggest dreams, the way my father had helped me, then I would be able one day to look in the mirror and give myself that *Babe* pat on the back. I'd be able to say, "That'll do, Michael."

It's a good check-in to have with yourself; outside of money, outside of career—is everything well in your home and your heart? Setting aside time to just spend with my family and friends did as much for my growth as anything else.

2. CHOOSE YOUR CONTRACTOR CAREFULLY

Anyone who has ever had a contractor run out on them or hired a project manager who couldn't keep the project on time and on budget knows how important it is to have someone capable running your team. Constance Schwartz was the first person I called when I retired. Having seen her in action at the NFL, having seen her run all of Snoop's business, I knew she'd be a great person to help me navigate the next stage of my career. She had vision and she understood how to negotiate big deals and manage people. But there are a lot of people who can do that. What set Constance apart then and now is that she is fiercely loyal to the people she has committed to. I thought, "Who's the one person I know who would put my interests first?" As selfish as that sounds, she honestly would put herself in harm's way to save me. I wouldn't want her to do it, of course. We're not remaking *The Bodyguard* or anything. But knowing how much she would protect me meant everything to me. I needed more than a manager. I needed a business partner whom I could trust like family.

A lot of people in the workplace talk about the importance of mentors. When I hear that, I often wonder if what they are looking for is a fairy godmother or fairy godfather—someone who's going to open doors and make the path easy. That's not been the experience of anyone I know. In Constance, I have not a mentor but a peer and a partner, someone with whom I can dream, with whom I can brainstorm and plan. The kind of friendship I have with Constance is something that all of us can cultivate in our own professional lives, and I believe that it is just as valuable, if not more so, than finding one specific mentor.

I can tell Constance anything. She always says, "If you tell me everything, I can help you. If you don't, then I can't." There are no secrets between us. When you're in the hunt to achieve your biggest dreams, what people in the corporate world call a BHAG—a Big Hairy Audacious Goal—you need to know that you have someone in your corner.

Just as you wouldn't start a major renovation without giving considerable thought to whom you'll select as your contractor, a person with whom you can discuss ideas, budgets, places to splurge, and places to compromise, don't approach your personal renovation without the right partner in your corner, not only encouraging you but also telling you the hard stuff, someone who will be brutally honest with you.

3. BE REALISTIC ABOUT YOUR TIMELINE

Renovating a home is a lesson in patience and compromise. You wouldn't expect to walk into a fixer-upper and then five days later have it somehow magically transformed into your dream home. In the same way, when you're renovating your life—overhauling your career or setting any other major life goal—make sure you give yourself enough time to get where you want to go.

I'm very close to my nephew Brett. I love him like my son. Brett's had his struggles, but he's worked hard and now he's in his twenties and has two jobs: he works at GNC and he works at Sunglass Hut. I joke that he sells everything I need: protein shakes and sunglasses. I know that he is anxious to get a shot at something bigger and better. When you work for an hourly wage, it can take two jobs just to keep food on the table, gas in the car, and a roof over your head. I encourage Brett to take the long view. "This is not for the rest of your life," I tell him. "Know where you want to go— that's where the visualization comes in—and keep building toward that dream and you will get there."

I remember those hourly wage jobs well, and I know the importance of having a vision and being able to execute it. When I was in high school and on vacations from college, I worked at the NCO (noncommissioned officers) Club in Mannheim, Germany, as a busboy and dishwasher. I'm telling you I have washed enough disgusting dirty dishes to last a lifetime. There were two cooks at the NCO Club. They had served in the military, and when they got out, they took jobs in the NCO kitchen. Every year the two would say, "I'm just doing this for one more year. I'm going to go back to school and get my college degree." And every year I'd come home from college and the two guys would be there, not happy, barely making a living, talking about "Just one more year and I'm getting out of here." It made such a huge impression on me because I thought, "I know one thing. I never want to be that person, stuck in rewind, always talking about next year but never making it happen."

Anyone who's ever had a renovation that goes on and on knows that you need to give yourself a timeline and a way to enforce it. Brett can't work indefinitely without a plan or his dreams will go unrealized, but at the same time he has to develop a strong work ethic as a foundation for his future goals. I like to give myself SMART goals:

- **S**pecific
- **M**easurable
- **A**ttainable
- **R**ealistic
- **T**ime-Bound

4. COPY WHAT WORKS

Whenever I'm renovating a house, I take great inspiration from visiting the homes of my friends. It's one thing to walk into a design store and see something that looks cool. It's a whole other thing to walk into someone's home and see an interesting design element and know that they've lived with it and it really works. One night I went to Mario Batali's house for dinner, and I saw that he and his wife had this metal slide built into their kitchen island in which they safely stored their knives. I immediately called my contractor and said, "Let's put in one of those."

I think the same philosophy applies in life. Tony Robbins said it best when he said, "Success leaves clues." From the days when I was reading Herschel Walker's workout book as a kid growing up in Germany, I have been looking at the lives of others to give me inspiration on how to shape and design my own. Funny story. When I was a chubby kid looking for inspiration to trim a few pounds so I could shed my moniker, "Bob," I discovered the book by Walker that I talk about in chapter 1. Years later, I actually had the opportunity to play with Walker before he retired. I played with him for the Giants, then against him when he played for the Eagles and the Cowboys. When I first met him, as an adult, I showed him the picture I'd taken with him as a kid.

I said, "I got this picture of you and me when I was thirteen in Germany."

He remembered the event, which had happened more than fifteen years before, perfectly. He said, "Oh yeah, that was the Polaroid promotion tour."

I said, "You know what that means? You're old."

He said, "Stop lying. Look at how big you are in that picture. You must have been twenty years old then," he teased, my weight adding a few years, no doubt.

Then I said, "Plus I bought your book. I just got to say, it didn't do anything for me and I want my money back."

He said, "Look at where you're at now! The book worked." He was *right*. The book did work.

My point is, don't think you have to reinvent the wheel. Look for role models in your field. Read their stories. Buy their books. Copy what works and make it your own.

5. BE WILLING TO ROLL UP YOUR SLEEVES AND DO THE WORK

There's an African proverb that says, "Move your feet while you pray." For me that means that after you've taken the time to architect your dreams, with all the meditation, visualization, and positive energy that entails, then you've got to switch gears and get into execution mode. Be forewarned, it's messy and unpredictable, and you never know what you'll find once you start taking down walls.

16

COME PREPARED

Rule #16

Dreams don't work unless you do.

AM ALWAYS SCARED. I was scared every time I put on a uniform and stepped on the field. I'm scared every time I put on a suit and step into a studio and walk onstage. I'm scared because I fear that I will not live up to what's expected. It's the way I'm built. I'm more afraid of failure than I am motivated by the accolades that come with success.

It goes back to Lou Gehrig. For a really long time, Lou Gehrig held the record for the most consecutive games played in baseball, which was an incredible record. Lou Gehrig got the job because Wally Pipp didn't want to play one day and decided that "Lou Gehrig could come fill in for me."

Most of us have never heard of Wally Pipp, because once Lou Gehrig stepped in, he never looked back, he never gave it up. They asked him, "Why do you play so hard every day?" The Major League Baseball schedule is demanding, brutal. He said, "Because there can be some kid who's watching, who came to his first baseball game, who's never heard of me, or may have heard of me and never seen me play, and this is his first experience. If I cheat on that day, I'm cheating that person whose first experience it is to watch."

That's how I feel about *LIVE with Kelly and Michael*. Every day that I'm lucky enough to step onto that stage, I think, "I've got an hour to give it one hundred percent. This could be somebody's first time. They've heard about this show. They're saying, 'What is the big stink? What is this stink about Michael, and *Kelly and Michael?*' They may have even saved up their money to travel to New York to see a variety of shows, including ours. Not wanting to disappoint others—to fail—that's what motivates me."

Being on television may seem like the easiest, most lucrative gig going, but for me, it was like being a rookie all over again. No one can really teach you how to be on television: they put the camera on you, they turn it on, and you sink or swim. Or more accurately, you sink, come up for air, dry yourself off, and then try again. When I first joined *NFL on FOX,* for the first three weeks, I was sure I was sinking. I was so scared and nervous. I remember thinking, "I should've gone back to the Giants for that extra year. I should've played football for as long as I could." I couldn't show it, but underneath the anchors' desk, my legs were shaking like a dog's tail. Then the second the camera was shut off, I'd turn to Jimmy Johnson, and ask, "Did I make any sense? Because I don't remember what I said just two seconds ago." But eventually I got the hang of it.

The *LIVE* show has always had a special place in television history and the hearts of the American viewers. Regis Philbin started with a show called *A.M. Los Angeles* in 1975, when I was four years old. Many of its predecessors, including *A.M. New York,* had been canceled by the early 1980s. Regis's show was a survivor. In 1983, Regis debuted in New York on a new WABC program called *The Morning Show with Regis and Cyndy Garvey*. In 1985, Kathie Lee Gifford joined the show and it became the number one show in the market. When it went national, it was renamed *Live with Regis and Kathie Lee*. Kelly joined the show in 2001, and for ten years, she and Regis were the dynamic duo, winning Daytime Emmys and millions of viewers in the process.

I took the history of *LIVE* seriously because I have so much respect for what an amazing broadcasting institution it was and is. After Regis Philbin retired in 2011, the show spent nearly a year auditioning for a new cohost for Kelly. I was one of those cohosts, but I was one of many. It was almost like being on *The Bachelor* and wondering who would get the rose because Kelly shared morning coffee with a *lot* of guys, including Seth Meyers, Josh Groban, Nick Lachey, and Neil Patrick Harris. Not to mention the amazing women who sat in as guest hosts, like Kristin Chenoweth, Lucy Liu, and Katie Couric.

For a long time, I wasn't favored or even thought to be a contender for the job. It was a familiar scenario. It was as if I'd shown up to play an away game at the Colts home stadium. Nobody's screaming "Strahan! Strahan!" in the crowd. I also knew that just because no one was screaming my name, it didn't mean that I couldn't win. Most of us count ourselves out waaaay too early. We assume we can't win because someone else is the favorite, or—even more important—everyone is saying that someone else is the favorite, that we shouldn't even try for the win. It's true. There are a lot of people who are born with or who are given certain advantages. But trust me when I tell you this, the game of life is a lot fairer than we often realize. Hard work and dedication can carry you a very long way. I know because I've seen it in my own life. Not just in my year of trying out for the *LIVE* show, but ever since I was a chubby kid who dreamed of being a professional athlete.

After I got my first opportunity to host *LIVE* I remember thinking, "I know I can do this. I just need to work harder and figure it out." I watched the other guest hosts as carefully as I used to watch the film of other players. I'd review my mental notes: "Okay, I like this about this person. I don't like when this other person does that." And, of course, I studied how Kelly made it look so effortless. It was the same process I used as a football player. I pieced together my game from different people on the field. I paid attention to the details.

I had more than one person say to me, early on in the *LIVE* process, "The network owned by Disney is never going to give this spot to a retired black football player. It's their crown jewel. It's nine o'clock in the morning. It's just not going to happen." I let them know, "Well, I'm glad you're not making the decision, because color doesn't define my career. If I don't get it, it's because I'm not the right talent, it just wasn't the right fit."

I was a guest host for *LIVE* a total of twenty times. Try to think about the last time you tried something twenty times, without any indication that it was going to pay off. For most of us, our days of trying new things just for the sake of the experience ends when we're kids. When was the last time you tried to learn a new language and showed up for twenty classes? When was the last time you tried to master a particularly tricky recipe and made the same dish over and over again, twenty times? Or picked up a tennis racket and went down to the court and said, "I'm going to do this twenty times this summer. Even though I've never really done it before." Many of us are so caught up in our day-to-day life, it's been a while since we've tried something new. And when we try and we don't knock it out of the park right away, we feel as if we've failed. We give up too soon.

If I walked into the studio thinking, "They're never going to pick a former pro football player to partner up with Kelly Ripa," then I would have never gotten the job. Instead, I came in with my best attitude each and every time. I enjoyed the job I had—being a guest host, for that one day—and I made an effort to excel not just for myself, but also for Kelly and the whole behind-the-scenes team.

After my twentieth time as a guest host, I was called upstairs. It felt as if I was in trouble and was being sent to the principal's office. I sat down with Dave Davis (president and general manager of WABC) and Michael Gelman (*LIVE* executive producer), and then Kelly walked in. She didn't say, "Okay, we're giving you the job." Her exact words were: "We want to know if you would do us the honor of considering taking over as a full-time host." I mean, she asked me in the nicest possible way, which meant so much, and says so much about her character as a person. I couldn't believe it. I said, "You had me at considering."

It's almost eerie for me to go back and look at that appearance I did on *Live with Regis and Kelly* in 2008 after I retired from the Giants. Regis asked me, "What are you going to do with the rest of your life? You've got a lot of personality, a lot of charisma." I said, "Well, there's a show that I'm on right now. Maybe you want to . . ." The audience burst out laughing. Regis said, "You never know who's going to sit here next." Then I said, *"LIVE with Kelly and Michael."* And Kelly said, "I like the sound of that." But honestly, I didn't remember saying that until I was shown the footage after they offered me the job. Somewhere deep down, I must've known. Or at least known that it was a job I would love to do.

My dad used to say you speak things into existence. When I get an idea that I want to do something, it's never a case of here are a hundred reasons why this can't happen. I always think, "It's going to happen, it's going to happen. It may not happen right now or exactly the way I'm thinking about it, but it'll happen." Watching that clip of me with Kelly and Regis reminds me of how powerful our thoughts and words are, how powerful it is to put a positive idea out in the world and watch it ricochet back to you.

It's not that I don't have my doubts; it's that I don't succumb to them. The whole first year of *LIVE* was a constant stream of new challenges and new fears. The first year I covered the Academy Awards, I was a nervous wreck. First of all, I don't have that ego where I expect that everybody knows who I am. I remember seeing all of those movie stars and thinking, "Are they going to come over here and talk to me?" Even the ones who had been on our show, are they going to think it's worth their time to come over? Kelly wasn't with me on the red carpet, so I was particularly nervous and felt exposed. I was asking myself, "Am I good enough to be by myself on air and do these one-on-one interviews?"

Feeling the pressure, there I was standing there, sweating in my tux, when I saw Robin Roberts. A familiar face. I thought, "Oh, thank God. You sent an angel, right when I needed it."

Robin came over to me and asked me off camera, "How are you doing?"

I was honest. I told her, "Basically, I'm scared out of my mind."

She said, "Hey, remember. I came from sports."

The second she said that I just thought, "You came from sports as I did and you're here. I've seen and respect everything you've done."

Robin took my hand and said, "Don't worry, Michael. You belong here."

Robin Roberts. I love that woman with my entire heart. When she said that to me, she put me at ease.

Robin was both a great comfort and a source of knowledge for me when I got the opportunity to be part of a show where real news is reported by a team of seasoned journalists. Joining the *Good Morning America* team brought a whole new level of challenge and fear to me. This was real news. I study George and Robin. I study Lara, Amy, and Ginger. I watch how they craft their technique, how they modulate their vocal tone according to the mood of the story they're reporting, how they use pauses for emphasis. I absolutely study and am in awe of how my colleagues make it look easy, because it's anything but.

I've emphasized throughout the book how essential it is to be prepared (try being underprepared when you're facing a three-hundred-pound opponent), but even that's not enough. You have to have the confidence to go for it. Sometimes even when we're prepared—we've done all the work, we've got the skills to pay the bills—we're *still* afraid to go for our dreams. In his book *The Big Leap,* Gay Hendricks writes about a trend he calls "Upper

Limiting." He explains it this way: "Think of it like a thermostat. If you have a thermostat in your house set to 60 degrees, the moment your house starts to get a little warmer—creeping up to 62, 64 degrees, what happens? The air conditioner kicks in and brings the temperature back to a chilly 60. A similar thing happens with the level of happiness, love, financial abundance, success, and creativity we experience in our lives. If our thermostats are set low, we have a tendency to sabotage ourselves as we bump up against our Upper Limits."

I saw this Upper Limiting phenomenon at play in the life of Ollie Stancil, one of my dearest friends. Ollie has been my barber for twenty-one years—almost half my life. He's about two years older than me and has always worked at a barbershop. Not too long ago, the woman who owned the shop he's been working in for over a decade announced she was shutting it down. Ollie was devastated. This was his livelihood. Both he and his wife worked there. The whole family income was about to be compromised, possibly gone in a single swoop.

He emailed me the news and we are started talking. I could tell he was really lost. He kept saying, "Why do I have to leave this shop? This is madness. The business is so good here. Why is she shutting down?"

One afternoon as he prepared to cut my hair, I asked him, "What are you going to do?"

He said, "I don't know. I guess I'll find a job at another shop."

I said, "Well, why don't just open your own shop?"

I could tell that the thought had never occurred to him. I could also tell he was frightened by the idea. He responded, "Well, you know, it's not easy making that rent every month. There's all of that overhead. And who's going to manage the books? I cut hair, I'm not an accountant . . ."

It was excuse after excuse after excuse.

I listened, and in a pause, the opening I was waiting for, I asked him, "Ollie, what's really scaring you?"

He said, "I can't take such a big risk when I've got a wife and kids to feed."

I said, "Okay, but you could probably feed them even better if you open your own shop. You know how to run a shop. Your boss has been an absentee owner for years. She didn't even live in the same state as the shop. She lived a four-hour flight away. You've been basically running her shop." Besides, Ollie had a slew of loyal clients, some rather heavy hitters, such as Chris Rock, as well as several professional athletes. Even if in the unlikely event their careers took a hit, they would still be good for a haircut!

I urged him to consider going into business for himself so he could feel more in control of his own destiny.

After weeks of back-and-forth, I said, "Hey, enough with the excuses."

No one was happier than me when Ollie told me that he was taking over the barbershop from his former boss. He'd arranged the financing and was ready to step into the big, scary adventure of being a business owner. The look in his eyes told me that not only was he thrilled, but he had finally overcome his own fears. He was ready to step into the space of being a business owner and he was ready to succeed. I could visualize him as a success from the get-go. But it took a while for *him* to see it.

Ollie's business has been open for eight months now, and the shop is doing well. He bought out the space from the previous owner and completely renovated it, and anytime you walk into the shop, you can see the pride that he has in the place. You can *feel* it the minute you open the door.

It's good when somebody you care about says, "Enough with the excuses. Enough." Ollie thinks he's surprised me by being such a good businessman. But the person he really surprised was himself. No matter what profession we are in, we hold ourselves back and doubt ourselves more than anybody else ever will. Like Kendrick Lamar says in that song, "Everybody lacks confidence." It's what we do when we feel this lack that determines the outcome of our lives.

Don't underestimate the power of nurturing a dream— especially if it's something that you've been building toward your whole life. Nobody wants to invest, hire, or help someone who says, "I had a dream but I let it die years ago." People want someone who's done the research, done the work, and is ready to go to the next level. We hear no so often that we think that rejection is the mode that most of the world is in. But the truth is, there are lot of people and companies out there who want to say yes. Saying yes creates possibility for everyone involved. And it feels good. It feels good to the person saying it and it feels good to the person hearing it. Everyone wants to be in the yes business.

17

THINK RICHLY

Rule #17

There's more power in your attitude than in your bank account.

T'S NO ACCIDENT that everyone on my team has one thing in common. A super-positive, glass-is-always-half-full attitude. They embody the one mantra that may well be more important to me than any other I've touched upon: *There's more power in your attitude than in your bank account.* There are so many people I count as positive team members, it's hard to single out just a couple, but Latreal "La" Mitchell's attitude shines so bright.

Having played professional football for fifteen years, I thought I was in fairly good shape. Bruised, yes. But in good shape. Then I got the call to appear in *Magic Mike XXL.* I read the script; I knew it would call for me to be ripped, and I had only a few weeks to do it. One of the things I've learned, as a Hollywood outsider looking in, at guys like Channing Tatum, Hugh Jackman, and Dwayne

Johnson, is how physically demanding their jobs really are. It's kind of funny, because here I am a professional athlete, and I look at Channing on set and he's doing things that I know would *hurt* me. There's nobody dancing and spending hours learning grueling choreography for Channing. He's not sleeping in his trailer and saying, "Wake me up when you need to see my face."

Hugh Jackman was also a huge inspiration as I began to prepare for my first big movie role. I remember meeting Hugh at the Super Bowl in Dallas. I was pretty sure that he didn't know me from Adam. I was and am such a Wolverine fan. He came over to me and started asking me questions about working out. I was so stunned, I thought, "What is Hugh asking me?" We're friends now, and I can tell you this guy works his tail off. He's incredibly intelligent and thoughtful, but he works hard at his fitness and his health because so much of his work requires a level of physical excellence. From serious theatrical roles on Broadway, to singing and dancing, to the big-budget movies, he does it all and it's not by accident. He's a guy who understands the importance of dedication and doing the work.

So how was I going to bring that same level of professionalism to prepare for *Magic Mike* in such a short time? From the beginning, my trainer convinced me that "we got this." The ability to be about it and not just talk about it is one of the things I love most about Latreal "La" Mitchell. Despite the fact that she has a pretty good job working with me, La is never satisfied with the status quo. She is always studying and training for new certifications, mastery over different specializations. She reads voraciously, everything from books about fitness to books about nutrition, and has taken courses on everything from biology to physiology and beyond. She's not content to just help people get in shape; she wants to know every little detail about how the body works, so she can help her clients achieve more but also stay safe and healthy. There's a Flywheel, a popular spin studio, in our office building. When I saw La leave the studio, I thought she had just finished a class. Well, she had, but it wasn't one to work off the previous night's dinner, it was one she was applying toward her certification as a Flywheel instructor. She's successful and inspiring because while a lot of people I know spend their "free time" binge-watching TV shows, La is using that time to make her dreams come true. I've got three jobs on television—*GMA, LIVE with Kelly and Michael,* and *NFL on FOX*—and even I can't match La's discipline and stamina.

How many times have I worked out with her and she's ready to go for another two hours just as I'm about to collapse? But her optimism about my reaching my goal (to say nothing of her strict diet—no caffeine other than green tea, no alcohol, no sugar, and no bread) not only sustained me but convinced me it was doable.

What makes her attitude so winning and inspirational is that she never asks me to do anything that she can't do. She works out a lot harder than I do. She's up as early if not earlier than I am, and she brings to her day everything she's got. It's an important lesson when you're trying to motivate the people around you—be it your spouse, your kids, your coworkers, or your friends: don't ask people to do something that you're not already stepping up to do yourself. People have to see that you're walking the walk.

La is a person who says yes far more often than she'll ever say no. Tina Fey calls it the "Rule of Agreement." It comes from the world of improv, and as Tina explains it:

The first rule of improvisation is agree. Always agree and say yes. When you're improvising, this means you are required to agree with whatever your partner has created. So if we're improvising and I say, "Freeze, I have a gun," and you say, "That's not a gun. It's your finger. You're pointing your finger at me," our improvised scene has ground to a halt. But if I say, "Freeze, I have a gun!" and you say, "The gun I gave you for Christmas! You bastard!" then we have started a scene because we have agreed that my finger is in fact a Christmas gun.

Now, obviously in real life you're not always going to agree with everything everyone says. But the Rule of Agreement reminds you to "respect what your partner has created" and to at least start from an openminded place. Start with a yes and see where that takes you.

The Rule of Agreement isn't just limited to improv; it's also what makes a sports team work together in absolute synchronicity, and, as I see it, it should apply to life. While it's such a simple concept, it seems like it can be a hard one for people to grasp. I see it on every level, from assistants to top execs; you ask them about something and their first answer is no. No, it can't be done. No, it's not possible. No, it's too expensive, too hard, will take too long, *whatever.* The people I like to work with follow Tina's attitude. They say yes and see where it takes them.

Take, for example, another member of our team, Jose Diaz. To us, he's someone who embodies the American dream. His parents were from Mexico, Spanish was his first language, and he worked while also going to college. He took on a ton of student loans to put himself through the University of Southern California. Then he's gay, which being the child of Mexican immigrants might not have gone over well, but his family was incredibly supportive of who he is and all he hoped to accomplish.

Initially he was hired as Constance's intern, and she saw something in him and made him her assistant. Jose is a can-do guy. Anything we threw at him, in those early years, he handled and he did so with grace, so much so that a catchphrase developed around our office, "Why don't you ask Jose?"

When I moved to New York for *LIVE*, I asked Constance if he could move to New York and be my day-to-day right hand. Now, he's our director of branding. I see in Jose the same inner strength and drive that every member of our team possesses. But more than that, he's got this can't-beat-it attitude. In the middle of all our production company chaos, he's our calm. He never adds to the problem. He's always the one with a solution.

One of the youngest people on our team, Sarah Politis, always says yes, and that attitude, alongside her positive demeanor, has taken her very far. If she's had a bad day or a bad night, I've never seen it. The energy of Sarah is the energy of happiness. When you put out the energy of being happy as opposed to being negative or sarcastic, bothered or needy, then you become a magnet. People want to be around you.

I met Sarah when she was in high school in Michigan. Already then she had so much initiative. She created a Web show and had, amazingly, managed to meet all kinds of interesting people: from Ford president and CEO Alan Mulally and the actor Drew Barrymore to the comedian Jeff Foxworthy and the swimmer Rebecca Soni, a six-time Olympic medalist. But when she approached me at an event for an interview, she didn't name-drop, she didn't try to impress me. She just approached me with the professionalism of a reporter who might work for FOX or ABC.

Some might say that Sarah is lucky; she's just out of school and she has a lot of responsibility in my management and production company, SMAC. But since so many of the people I've hired and come to call friends share Sarah's attitude, I know that any luck she's had, she's made. In their book *Get Lucky: How to Put Planned Serendipity to Work for You and Your Business,* the authors, Thor Muller and Lane Becker, identified eight skills necessary to create luck:

1. **FOSTER CONDITIONS FOR SERENDIPITY AND ATTRACT IT.** Sarah did that by creating her own Web series. She wasn't just asking celebrities for autographs; she created a platform to share the interviews she was conducting.

2. **MAXIMIZE PHYSICAL MOVEMENT IN THE WORKPLACE.** If you've ever seen my business partner Constance in action, you would understand why I call her a force of nature. She's never been someone to sit behind a desk all day. She's up and about, talking to people, reading, researching, observing. She's successful because she's up and at it every day. She never dials it in.

3. **PREPARATION.** I learned this as an athlete, but I've practiced it and honed it in my life now in television. I always do my homework. I study the tapes and I come prepared.

4. **DIVERGENCE.** The authors define this as making goals that allow for changing circumstances. Remember when I had that television show *Brothers,* and it was canceled? I shifted gears and began exploring the options that led to me being on *LIVE.* Divergence.

5. **ACTIVATION.** The authors define this as "creating new activities to open up awareness of all the possibilities." I see this so clearly in my trainer, La. She's always pursuing new activities and creating new possibilities in the process.

6. **CONNECTION.** The authors talk about the importance of not only making a multiplicity of connections but nurturing those connections so that they have a deep quality. I see this in people like my friend Artie Rabin, who's an extraordinary entrepreneur, and Dr. Ian Smith, who does everything from books to TV. They don't just network for networking's sake. They really care about people and have friendships and work relationships that last for decades as a result.

7. **PERMEABILITY.** In their book, the authors discuss this as having an open exchange of information. This is something I live and breathe. I believe a great idea can come from anywhere. I'm as excited to hear pitches from twentysomethings as I am to go to lunch with smart people who are in their sixties and seventies. Our luck is directly related to our ability to find ideas and inspiration everywhere we go.

8. **ATTRACTION.** The last "get lucky" quality the authors identify is attraction, which they define as "projecting your purpose out in the world." This is what I get from my visualization time. It's what I share with my kids and my nephew. If you can dream it, you can achieve it.

I read a story once about a photographer who was trying to buy his dream house. It was an old house in the country, owned by a family friend. The owner knew that the photographer didn't have enough money to buy the house, so he gave him two years to come up with the money before he put the house on the market. For two years, he said yes to every assignment that was offered to him. If a toilet bowl company wanted him to take pictures of toilet bowls for their catalogue, he said yes, because he needed the money, he wanted to buy this house: it was everything he had ever dreamed of. He said, "For those two years, I was never so happy to go to work. Everything I photographed was beautiful to me, even when it was actually something really ugly. Because when I lifted up the camera and looked through the lens, I saw my dream house."

That story has stuck with me because, in so many ways, it's a powerful metaphor for how we can harness the power of a great attitude to make our dreams come true. Wayne Dyer says, "When you change the way you look at things, the things you look at change." I've seen this in my own life. I saw it in my father's journey. I see it now as I watch my friends drive toward their greatest dreams. It's the reason I truly believe that there's more power in your attitude than in your bank account.

18

WAKE UP HAPPY

Rule #18

Navigate your life as if it were a Ferrari. The more you process your observations, your opportunities, *and* your failures—and the more you take time to adjust—the smoother your ride will be.

T'S TAKEN TIME for me to get there, but more and more, I view my life like a car. Not like the Festiva I bought without testing it back in the day; but like one of those modern ones with built-in computers that recalibrate every few miles, the kind that are truly aware of the road and how to take a bump. The older I get, the more I know how to absorb the impact of a big pothole, how to get over it without denting the rim.

It's like the time in college when I returned to Germany for winter break and I wanted my dad to give me a job and make life easier so I didn't have to go back to college, where I was lonely and homesick. My dad could and did counsel me, but he couldn't do the growing up for me. I had to do it on my own, and I'm still doing it—the growing up, the fine-tuning never stops. A lot of people think, "Oh, if you're well known, and if you're on television, people make life easier for you." In truth, I've learned that the inside work you still have to do yourself.

At twenty-one, I defined happiness as having a job, making good money, being drafted, feeling that when people looked at me they thought, "Oh, look at him! He's the big football player. He's successful. He's the man!" Happiness was making a play on the football field and having the crowd cheer. It was about holding my insecurities at bay while I fed my ego.

In my thirties, I was still focused on accomplishments, but also increasingly on the people around me. My happiness increased if the people around me were happy, if they felt safe and secure, if they felt proud. I first became a father when I was in my twenties, but in my thirties, I understood my role as a father so much more. I began to realize that my world was a lot bigger than just me. I started to understand that what I did was a reflection of everybody attached to me; I affected more people than just myself. Happiness is about enjoying those different aspects of your life that you started developing in your twenties, and doing so with your family and friends.

Now, in my forties, happiness has become more about enjoying each step of the ride. That's why waking up happy, working for my happiness on a day-to-day basis, means so much to me. I was always told "Work hard when you're young so you can enjoy it when you're older." But in my view, we should really be enjoying it all the way through. We shouldn't just say, "Well, let me be miserable now, and later, when I retire, when I have X amount in the bank, then I'll be happy." You've got to learn to find the joy all the way through your life and not look at happiness as an end point.

A Princeton University study showed that once family income tops $75,000, happiness tends to plateau. Below $75,000, as many people know, life can be and often is a struggle. But the researchers were surprised to find that there was no big happiness spike between those who made $75,000 or $100,000 and those who made $100,000 and $200,000. In fact, increased income often came with greater pressures and a greater degree of stress and unhappiness. Don't get me wrong, I know that making a six-figure income can be a lovely thing. But if you've spent even an hour watching reality TV or reading celebrity tabloids, you know that money can't and doesn't buy happiness. It pays, emotionally as well as financially, to approach each day with the attitude that happiness is a moving target. There's always another mountain to climb, another hurdle to overcome. The playwright August Wilson once said that the key to being happy is to get yourself a little cup. If you walk around with a bucket, you'll never keep it filled. But a little cup is easy to fill. I fill my cup with moments like playing cards with my family and eating my mom's home cooking. I will spend hours playing cards with my parents and extended family, and there is no place I'd rather be.

We can always achieve more in the future. And I'm an ambitious person. I always have big plans. But what I've learned is that 99 percent of happiness isn't about achieving more in the future. It's about *being* more in the present. Moment to moment. Day to day. Waking up happy, and when we don't wake up happy, doing everything in our power to get there. As I showed in chapter 2, it's about the journey toward your goal.

As I get older, I'm learning that the only opinion that matters and the only thing that's going to help me get better is the faith I have in myself. I've learned that I control my confidence level. I control my happiness. I control my attitude. These aren't based on somebody else's opinion. They aren't based on somebody else's truth. They're based on my truth.

I've got four amazing children. I'm surrounded by the most loyal, funny, inspiring friends. I no longer wake up on Sunday mornings wondering if today is the day that a 340-pound offensive lineman is going to break some critical bone in my body and end my football career. I no longer have to physically punish myself in the name of sports glory. Most days, I wake up in a city I love, walk across a park I love—one that happens to be one of the most gorgeous in the world, Central Park—to a job I love, with colleagues I admire. My job is to talk and listen to some of the most interesting people in the world and in-between segments interact with members of the audience who come from all walks of life. I've got it good. But I've also worked hard (really hard—not kinda hard, but really hard) to make this life for myself.

I'm constantly working on myself, constantly trying to figure out who I am, what I like, what I don't like, where I think I am, and where I want to go. I'm constantly assessing what makes me happy, what doesn't make me happy. It's kind of like how they build these modern cars. You hear about these Ferraris, and you think, "Why does this car cost $300,000? Why does this Rolls-Royce cost $350,000? How can they cost this much when I can get a Honda for $17,500?" But to ride in a Ferrari or to drive a Rolls-Royce is to understand why. Those cars are like supercomputers that constantly calculate and readjust every 0.30 milliseconds to give you the smoothest ride possible. So I try to navigate my life as if it were a Ferrari. The more conscious I am, the more I process the information I'm given and readjust based on what I've learned, the smoother my ride in life becomes.

You too should navigate your life as if it were a Ferrari. The more conscious you are, the more you process your observations, your opportunities, *and* your failures, and the more you take time to adjust—the smoother your ride will be.

It's my greatest hope that something in this book becomes a tool that helps you take your life and your dreams to the next level. Deepak Chopra has said that "we are all millionaires with amnesia." By this, he means that we forget that life itself is a truly wondrous gift. I believe that each of our lives is as precious and as amazing as a Ferrari. It's your life. Drive it like you own it. Because you do.

EPILOGUE:
MOTIVATED TO FIND LOVE

N O MATTER HOW you define your goals, it seems to me, you can claim you've achieved them only once you have someone with whom you can share that victory. That tribe includes friends, family, and, optimally, a partner as well. I've got the first two nailed down—a group of loyal friends and the best family anyone could ask for. But as I wrote earlier, a Google search will quickly reveal how I'm still working on that special someone.

Professional athletes aren't often thought of as relationship experts. I get it. I've been divorced twice. But believe it or not, my friends and I spend a lot of time talking not just about women but about relationships and love. I think at the end of the day, every guy just want to be with somebody who understands him. I don't think anybody except for a Hugh Hefner wannabe really wants to be that eighty-year-old guy surrounded by twenty-year-old girls.

When I say that I'm not perfect, that I'm a student of life and that fear of failure drives me, some people assume that I'm being falsely humble. But if there's an area where one can see that I'm a work in progress, it's my love life. I was always the guy who wanted to be married, who wanted to be the football player who came home to his wife and kids. It didn't happen that way, obviously, as both of my marriages ended in divorce. But that doesn't mean I've given up on love—on the contrary. For me, figuring out how to find a true, long-lasting love is like trying to figure out how to get to the Super Bowl when your team has lost season after season. It's another instance of improbable, not impossible. Just because it hasn't happened yet doesn't mean it won't happen in the future. As you can tell by now, I'm a guy who constantly rewinds the tape, studying my own path and the paths of others. In the process, I've observed a few things and made a few goals. Here's what have I observed from all those years reviewing the tape of my own romantic mistakes:

1. **GUYS LIKE THE CHASE.** We respect somebody who challenges us. That's what the thrill of the chase is all about. Here's an analogy: If you see something that is expensive and out of reach, you process it along these lines: "I want that. How long would it take for me to attain that? I am going to get that!" Once you get it, you take care of it. It is precious. It matters to you, and the more work you put in to get it, the less willing you are to give it up so easily, so quickly. But if you see something and it's easily attainable, you're likely to be careless with it. The same is true for relationships.

2. **PHYSICAL ATTRACTION GOES ONLY SO FAR.** There's no denying it—men put a lot of emphasis on looks. We know from the instant we meet somebody whether we're attracted to them physically. That's the easy part. It's the soul chemistry that takes more time to figure out. After a date or two, we guys think we

know whether or not our personalities are compatible with a woman's. But increasingly, as I mature, I'm starting to wonder if we're all too affected by how disposable our culture has become. Some treat relationships like an iPhone, something you update every time a new model is available. Or, say, a coffee cup. Nowadays you have your coffee and throw the cup away. Back in the day, you would carry around a thermos, take it home and clean it out. You kept it forever. Now we're such a disposable society, we've even begun to think of our relationships that way. We men eventually get around to slowing down and realizing not everything is disposable, but only after we've matured a bit.

3. **MYSTERY IS SEXY.** One of the easiest ways to get a first date off on the wrong foot is to tell your whole life story in the first twenty-five minutes. There is nothing sexier than a little mystery.

4. **MEN LISTEN MORE THAN WE'RE GIVEN CREDIT FOR.** People think men don't talk enough, but that's because we listen more than we are given credit for. We ask questions because we're trying to pick up little pieces of information about you. By listening, we can piece together a woman's life—her attitude, her feelings, where she is in her life. By listening, we piece together a personality, the story of who this person is and who she might become.

Here's the rub: as much as we enjoy listening, if a woman talks and talks, but doesn't ask any questions, it gets boring very quickly. While we're piecing together her story, we want her to show that she thinks we're interesting as well.

It has to be a two-way conversation. If it's a one-way conversation, in his head the guy's probably saying, "I can't wait to get out of here because she won't stop talking!"

If I don't get a word in on a date, then I am looking for the exit. Like my friend Jay says, I will get the check, call her an Uber, and then I'm out. Because I know if I start a relationship with this woman, I will wake up to talking and I will go to sleep to talking. I can imagine myself driving around the neighborhood just so I don't have to enter the apartment.

5. **WE AVOID HIGH-MAINTENANCE WOMEN.** We want a woman who looks good. That's the first thing that attracts us. But we want her to look good in a way that can be casual and spontaneous. So if we say, "Hey, just throw on some sweats and let's go to a movie," she can do it and still look great. We like women who are flexible and confident enough to stand in their natural beauty. No man likes a woman with too much makeup on. That's too much commotion, too much maintenance.

Once I was on vacation in Mexico with a few friends, one of whom had this girlfriend who took forever to get ready. Every night, we were all late for dinner because we had to wait for her to glop on all this lipstick, makeup, and perfume. She was trying to be perfect; meanwhile, all I could think was "Relax. We're on vacation in Mexico." The ironic thing was that she was prettier without makeup, but she just couldn't see it.

Most days don't involve luxurious experiences. Most days *do* include hanging out in jeans or sweats, running errands or doing casual things such as going to a movie. That's real life. There are women with swag who are extremely sexy even when they're very casually dressed. It's just the persona, the aura that they give off, and that's what we're drawn to.

6. **SWAGGER IS A PHEROMONE.** We love women who are confident because they're good at something. Success is very sexy. Men

shouldn't be intimidated by it. A smart man shouldn't be intimidated by a woman with a career.

7. **LEARN TO ACCEPT A COMPLIMENT.** How a woman reacts to a compliment teaches us so much about who a woman really is. If I pay a woman a compliment and she deflects it, then she's probably not comfortable in receiving compliments. She probably doesn't see herself the way that I do—and that lack of confidence is very revealing. Unfortunately, far too many women just aren't comfortable in their skin. If you offer a simple "Oh, you're really pretty" or "You're funny" or "You're so talented"—they ooze discomfort. It's a fine balance. We want a woman to look us in the eye after we've said something nice about her and nod confidently.

8. **PERFECTION IS BORING.** Women get too caught up with being perfect. Perfect isn't real and it isn't interesting. First of all, what is perfect? Perfect to everybody is different. The greatest memories that I have are the mistakes, the things that I laugh at.

I remember the unusual, the spontaneous, and the unexpected, not the so-called perfect. When I played a great football game, I never left the stadium thinking. "Oh, man. That one move I made was perfect." I left the game and said, "Man, when that one play happened, I never saw it coming, but then I did this to counteract it. I'll remember and utilize it next time I'm in a pinch."

A woman may go through a lot of trouble to plan the "perfect evening," but odds are the guy may go home at the end of the night and say, "That was one boring date."

I really love that movie *The Best Man Holiday,* and one of the reasons is that it doesn't glorify perfection. A video of one of the guys' wives surfaces. It turns out that when she was in college, she took money for sex at a fraternity party. You expect to find out that it really wasn't his wife, it was mistaken identity or nothing really happened behind the closed door. Instead she says, "I'm sorry, I was young and dumb and I needed the money."

He responds by saying, "I love you and it happens." Of course, it's a movie, but the point is we are all flawed. Get over it!

9. **SOFT TRUMPS EDGE.** My business partner Constance spent much of her career as a female exec in the NFL. To date Constance, you had to be a strong man, because she applied, in my opinion, the toughness she used to get ahead in business to her dating life. She was a woman who was used to being in control, running her life, doing what she wanted to do when she needed to do it. It was very intimidating for men.

She'd no sooner have a guy than she would test him. And they all failed until she met Mike, now her husband. He was strong enough to call the test out for what it was.

I understand our softness is the most precious thing we can share with anybody and it renders us vulnerable. What's true for Constance is true for me, and most everyone I know. No one is truly comfortable being in a position of vulnerability. It's hard to get comfortable when you feel like somebody else has access to your deepest emotions. We've all had things that have happened to us throughout our lives that prevent us from letting others in; we're afraid that one day that person may use that vulnerability against us. Been there. Done that. But I don't intend to be cynical about love. I guard against the cynicism *and* work on letting the hurt feelings go.

10. **WILL YOU STILL LOVE ME WHEN I'M 92?** When I think of people who have great relationships, I think of my friends Peter and Stacy Hochfelder. Peter is one of the nicest people you could ever be around. He and his wife are like a newlywed couple. They met on a blind date. They even named their boat *Blind Date.* They always make sure that they are affectionate and romantic with and toward each other. The relationship makes them happy. They wake up happy and then spend their days nurturing that relationship.

Jocular, fun people, Peter and Stacy are as playful with each other now as they were at the beginning of their marriage twenty-six years ago. They remind me of my parents. They can't live without each other. I figured out only recently that when I'm talking to my mom, my dad is always on the phone. One day I called her in Texas and started talking mess about my dad. My mother, mind you, did not stop me. Then my father pipes up with "I'm on the phone." Thanks, Mom.

Mom and Dad, Peter and Stacy—those are my examples.

. . .

As I put into practice the ideas I've explored in this book, I know my sense of satisfaction will only grow deeper once I find that one person with whom I can do or say anything without feeling judged. In return, I'd like to provide a similar haven for her. Perhaps a relationship that is unconditional and nonjudgmental is as elusive as a Super Bowl ring, but that doesn't mean I won't try.

I'm learning how I want to feel in life. I'm learning how I want to feel in a relationship. I'm learning, again, as I did in Texas, a newly arrived kid from Germany, how to be by myself sometimes. More and more, I take walks in Central Park by myself. I go to a movie by myself. I'm learning that I need to be comfortable by myself. It's only going to help me learn to be comfortable with somebody else.

In August Wilson's play *Seven Guitars,* one of the main characters talks about what he's looking for in a relationship. He says, "I get me three rooms and a place to have a little garden and I'll be all right. Three rooms and a woman know how to sit with me in the dark, what else can a man want?"

It's what I call being comfortable. You don't have to say anything, but occasionally you look over and catch a little glimpse, a glance of the eye, and that's what matters. I want to come home, lay my head on her lap, have her rub my back while I lie there, still and at peace. I want that "Baby, why don't you come here and sit on the couch with me" kind of love. The sweetness of knowing "We don't have to talk, we can just be still." I talk enough in my day job!

ACKNOWLEDGMENTS

AM A REFLECTION of the incredible people who have supported me, encouraged me, and believed in me over the years.

I am humbled by the opportunity to share some of the lessons I have learned in my life in hopes of offering the same support, encouragement, and belief that all of YOU are capable of living your dreams like I am living mine.

To my parents, Gene and Louise, thank you for supporting my every endeavor. You've taught me to cherish my roots and honor my wings. All that I have achieved is because you instilled in me that anything is possible. You did not raise me to believe that I was worth my dreams, but that my dreams were worth me. You continue to be and always will be my biggest role models in life. Thank you for your infinite love.

To my kids, Tanita, Michael Jr., Sophia, and Isabella, thank you for your neverending love and encouragement. You've taught me to stay young, to look at things with innocent eyes, and to always have fun. Sometimes life is harder than you expect and things happen that are out of our control, but you never lose your spark for life.

Thank you for adding so much light to mine. I am so proud to be your father and to watch you grow into the incredible people that you are. Everything I do is for you.

To Jay Glazer, for being my best friend through the good and the bad, my rights and my wrongs, the highs and the lows. You have always had my back and I will always have yours. I've learned a lot from you about loyalty, friendship, and love.

To Constance Schwartz, who I consider my sister, my best friend, my sounding board, my business partner, and the boss, there are not enough pages in this book to truly express my gratitude for all that you have done for me over the years. You are a guiding light and the captain of my career. But most importantly, you are one of my dearest friends, and for that I am thankful.

To the rest of my SMAC Entertainment team, Jose Diaz, Sarah Politis, Tim Cullen, and Koral Chen. I appreciate all of your hard work and dedication to helping me be the best that I can be every day. Your early mornings and late nights do not go unnoticed.

To the people who have made my transition into television a pleasure:

My FOX family—

David Hill, Ed Goren, Eric Shanks, Bill Richards

Jimmy Johnson, Howie Long, Curt Menefee, Terry Bradshaw

My ABC family—

Bob Iger, Ben Sherwood, Rebecca Campbell, Dave Davis, Barbara Fedida, Janice Marinelli, Michael Gelman, Michael Corn, James Goldston, Tom Cibrowski

Kelly Ripa

Robin Roberts, George Stephanopoulos, Lara Spencer, Amy Robach, Ginger Zee

To Eric Simonoff and the WME team, thank you for connecting me to the right people to tell my story, my way. I appreciate all of your guidance.

Dawn Davis, your creativity and enthusiasm for this book was inspiring and motivational throughout this journey. Thank you and 37 INK, along with Judith Curr at Atria Books, for bringing this book to the world. I know there were a lot of behind-the-scenes people. I want to offer a special thanks to all of you, especially to production editor Isolde Sauer.

Veronica Chambers, thank you for helping me share my story. Your knowledge and experience was instrumental in this process and you made me dig deep to find my voice and were essential in bringing the essence of my stories to the pages.

And, finally, I want to thank everybody mentioned in the book because without all of you, there is no story to be told. I am eternally grateful for your friendship. You all have a special place in my heart, my soul, and in my being.

APPENDIX A: STRAHAN'S RULES

Rule #1

Help can—and will—come from the most unexpected places. Be open to everything around you.

Rule #2

Sometimes you'll catch the big fish, and sometimes you won't, but without a line in the water, you don't stand a chance.

Rule #3

Grit, desire, and discipline are free and the only equipment you need to start just about any endeavor you'll set out to do.

Rule #4

It's natural to have doubts. But hit pause before you out-and-out quit.

Rule #5

Too many of us count ourselves out before we even give ourselves a chance. Do the work. Be excellent. You'll find your place, and it may just be where you least expect it.

Rule #6

The juice is worth the squeeze. When we push ourselves, sometimes it hurts. But when we realize we've got more to give, we put ourselves in the position of getting more.

Rule #7

Ask yourself, "Am I the man or the woman that I hoped to be?" If you want to *be* more, then you've got to *do* more.

Rule #8

Play is the business of adults. Plato said, "You can discover more about a person in an hour of play than in a year of conversation."

Rule #9

Not if but when. The secret to success lies not in luck but in the things you do every day.

Rule #10

Though it's hard to appreciate this when you're going through a painful passage, it's the bad experiences that often teach you the most.

Rule #11

You can't change other people, but you can change how you are around them, and sometimes, a lot of times, that's more than enough.

Rule #12

Listen to other people, but don't take their opinions for fact. Have your own experiences. Draw your own conclusions.

Rule #13

Too late is in the grave . . . The decade ahead might hold more possibility than we previously imagined.

Rule #14

If you can dream it, you can achieve it. Use visualization to access it.

Rule #15

Don't approach your personal renovation without the right partner in your corner, not only encouraging you but also telling you the hard stuff, someone who will be brutally honest with you.

Rule #16

Dreams don't work unless you do.

Rule #17

There's more power in your attitude than in your bank account.

Rule #18

Navigate your life as if it were a Ferrari. The more you process your observations, your opportunities, *and* your failures—and the more you take time to adjust—the smoother your ride will be.

APPENDIX B:
SUGGESTED READING

1. *Herschel Walker's Basic Training* by Herschel Walker
2. *Before Happiness: The 5 Hidden Keys to Achieving Success, Spreading Happiness and Sustaining Positive Change* by Shawn Achor
3. *Service: A Navy SEAL at War* by Marcus Lutrell with James D. Hornfischer
4. *Headslap: The Life and Times of Deacon Jones* by John Klawitter and Deacon Jones
5. *It's Only a Game* by Terry Bradshaw with David Fisher
6. *The Happiness Project* by Gretchen Rubin
7. *The Power of Music: Pioneering Discoveries in the New Science of Song* by Elena Mannes
8. *Journey to the Heart: Daily Meditations on the Path to Freeing Your Soul* by Melody Beattie
9. *Body Intelligence: Harness Your Body's Energies for Your Best Life* by Joseph Cardillo, PhD
10. *What Should I Do with My Life?* by Po Bronson
11. *A More Beautiful Question: The Power of Inquiry to Spark Breakthrough Ideas* by Warren Berger
12. *The Big Leap: Conquer Your Hidden Fear and Take Life to the Next Level* by Gay Hendricks
13. *Bossypants* by Tina Fey

14. *Get Lucky: How to Put Planned Serendipity to Work for You and Your Business* by Thor Muller and Lane Becker

15. *Super Shred: The Big Results Diet* by Ian K. Smith, MD

16. *The Joy of Doing Things Badly: A Girl's Guide to Love, Life, and Foolish Bravery* by Veronica Chambers

17. *Flow: The Psychology of Optimal Experience* by Mihaly Csikszentmihalyi

APPENDIX C:
THE PLAYLIST

This playlist is a collection of uplifting songs that will help open your eyes. Whether you like rap, club music, classic pop, or oldies, there is something here for you. These songs will move you physically, emotionally, and mentally. I'm always looking for new music, so tweet me your favorite Wake Up Happy songs with the #wakeuphappy to @michaelstrahan.

1. "Lovely Day"—Bill Withers
2. "Rolling in the Deep"—Adele
3. "New York State of Mind"—Billy Joel
4. "Happy"—Pharrell Williams
5. "Locked Out of Heaven"—Bruno Mars
6. "New Flame"—Chris Brown
7. "The Man"—Aloe Blacc
8. "Square One"—Coldplay
9. "GO!"—Common
10. "Brown Sugar"—D'Angelo
11. "Doin' It Right"—Daft Punk
12. "I Can't Go for That (No Can Do)"—Hall & Oates
13. "Without You"—David Guetta featuring Usher
14. "Must Be the Money"—Deion Sanders
15. "Hello Good Morning"—Diddy

16. "You Know You Like It"—DJ Snake and AlunaGeorge

17. "A Song for You"—Donny Hathaway

18. "Forgot About Dre"—Dr. Dre

19. "0 to 100"—Drake

20. "September"—Earth Wind & Fire

21. "Lose Yourself"—Eminem

22. "Ready or Not"—Fugees

23. "Ain't Worried About Nothin"—French Montana

24. "Sussudio"—Phil Collins

25. "Midnight Train to Georgia"—Gladys Knight and The Pips

26. "I Like"—Guy

27. "Radioactive"—Imagine Dragons

28. "Caravan of Love"—The Isley Brothers

29. "Crooked Smile"—J. Cole

30. "Holy Grail"—Jay-Z

31. "F*ckwithmeyouknowigotit"—Jay-Z

32. "Run This Town"—Jay-Z

33. "Come & Talk to Me"—Jodeci

34. "Ordinary People"—John Legend

35. "Daughters"—John Mayer

36. "La Camisa Negra"—Juanes

37. "Through the Wire"—Kanye West

38. "Dancing on the Ceiling"—Lionel Richie

39. "Momma Said Knock You Out"—LL Cool J

40. "Livin' on a Prayer"—Bon Jovi

41. "Sexual Healing"—Marvin Gaye

42. "Sumthin' Sumthin' "—Maxwell

43. "I'll Be There for You (You're All I Need)"—Method Man featuring Mary J. Blige

44. "Rock with You"—Michael Jackson

ABOUT THE AUTHOR

Legendary Super Bowl Champion Michael Strahan recently earned an Emmy as cohost of the popular morning talk show *LIVE with Kelly and Michael*. He is also an analyst for *NFL on FOX*, for which he has received an Emmy nomination. Additionally, Strahan serves as special cohost for ABC's top-rated morning program, *Good Morning America*. Behind the scenes, he creates and produces films and programming as the cofounder of SMAC Entertainment, a management, branding, and production company.

Prior to joining the ranks of the top broadcasters in the country, Strahan's entire fifteen-year football career was typified by the charisma and sportsmanship that made him a seven-time Pro-Bowler and one of only four players ever to lead the NFL in sacks for two seasons. His spectacular NFL career resulted in Strahan being named to the 2014 class of the Pro Football Hall of Fame, the sport's highest honor.

Dedicated to many charitable works, Strahan donates his hands and heart to numerous charities, including St. Jude Children's Hospital, the USO, and HELP USA.

Born in Houston, Texas, Strahan spent most of his youth in Germany, where his father, Gene, was stationed in the US Army. He now divides his time between Los Angeles and New York and can be reached via Twitter @michaelstrahan.